Praise for Stephanie Danler's

Stray

A *Bustle*, *InStyle*, *Good Housekeeping*,
and Elle.com Best Book of the Year

A *BookPage* Best Memoir of the Year

"Stephanie Danler knows about the long-term damage of substance abuse in the family, how the trauma can manifest itself
decades later, and how recovery is never out of the cards. . . . A
reflective redemption story told from experience."
—*San Francisco Chronicle*

"Now that *Stray* is out in the world, the author has finally laid
claim to her biggest secret: her story of origin. No performances,
other than the ones used to craft a story with a beginning, middle and end. Just her feelings on the surface, in something as
intricate as lace but much more durable." —*Los Angeles Times*

"Stunning prose. . . . Danler tells her story candidly. . . . The
honesty she brings to her reader allows us to think about our
own story, the parts that make up a whole without trying to fit
our identity into a preordained box." —*Electric Lit*

"[*Stray* is] fearless, insightful, devastating, and beautiful. It broke my heart, and it twisted up my insides. The stories are still sitting in my gut. . . . Danler writes (beautifully, achingly) about the family she comes from and the one she's created for herself."
—Laura Marie Meyers, PopSugar

"Forceful, eviscerating. . . . Precise, elegant prose. . . . A penetrating and unforgettable tale of family dysfunction."
—*Publishers Weekly* (starred review)

"[A] fierce, unsparing memoir. . . . In Danler's evocation of California's complicated history and the darkness that lurks under its sunny exterior, *Stray* brings to mind the work of Joan Didion, and her frank portrayal of the nightmare of addiction is akin to Leslie Jamison's *The Recovering.* But in its painful candor and hard-earned wisdom, *Stray* is every bit its own vivid creation."
—*BookPage* (starred review)

"Acknowledging both the tribute of memory and the mercy of forgetting with one distinctive voice, this is a rare and skillfully structured view of an artist's love, grief, and growth."
—*Booklist*

"Danler's first memoir is as well-written as her novel was. . . . [A] moving text in which writing is therapeutic and family trauma is useful material."   —*Kirkus Reviews*

Stephanie Danler

Stray

Stephanie Danler is a novelist and screenwriter. She is the author of the international bestseller *Sweetbitter* and the creator and executive producer of the *Sweetbitter* TV series. Her work has appeared in *The Sewanee Review*, *Vogue*, *The New York Times Book Review*, and *The Paris Review Daily*. She lives in Los Angeles, California.

www.stephaniedanler.com

ALSO BY STEPHANIE DANLER

Sweetbitter

Stray

Stray

A MEMOIR

Stephanie Danler

VINTAGE BOOKS
A DIVISION OF PENGUIN RANDOM HOUSE LLC
NEW YORK

FIRST VINTAGE BOOKS EDITION, APRIL 2021

The Library of Congress has cataloged the Knopf edition as follows:
Names: Danler, Stephanie, author.
Title: Stray : a memoir / by Stephanie Danler.
Description: First edition. | New York : Alfred A. Knopf, 2020.
Identifiers: LCCN 2019055034 (print) | LCCN 2019055035 (ebook)
Subjects: LCSH: Danler, Stephanie. | Authors, American—21st century—
Biography. | Women authors, American—20th century—Biography.
| Children of alcoholics—California—Biography. | Children of drug
addicts—California—Biography.
Classification: LCC PS3604.A5376 Z46 2020 (print) | LCC PS3604.A5376
(ebook) | DDC 813/.6 B—dc23
LC record available at https://lccn.loc.gov/2019055034
LC ebook record available at https://lccn.loc.gov/2019055035

Vintage Books Trade Paperback ISBN: 978-1-101-91187-7
eBook ISBN: 978-1-101-87597-1

Book design by Cassandra J. Pappas

www.vintagebooks.com

Printed in the United States of America
10 9 8 7 6 5 4 3 2 1

To Matthew and Julian Wild.

The end of this story and the beginning of the next.

Now I am quietly waiting for
the catastrophe of my personality
to seem beautiful again,
and interesting, and modern.

The country is grey and
brown and white in trees,
snows and skies of laughter
always diminishing, less funny
not just darker, not just grey.

It may be the coldest day of
the year, what does he think of
that? I mean, what do I? And if I do,
perhaps I am myself again.

—FRANK O'HARA, "Mayakovsky"

I have been looking all my life for
history and have yet to find it.

—JOAN DIDION, *South and West*

Contents

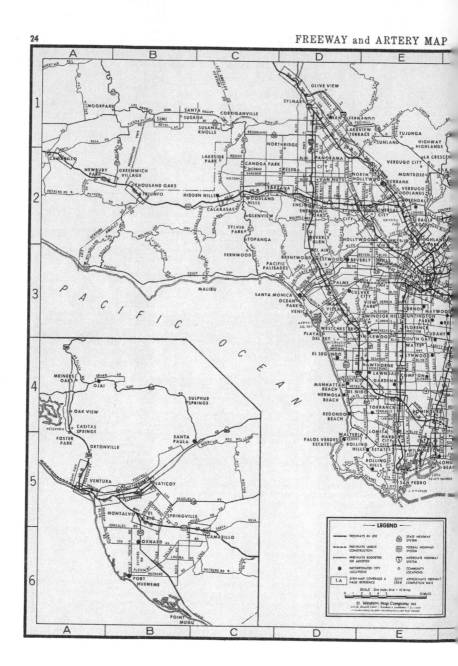

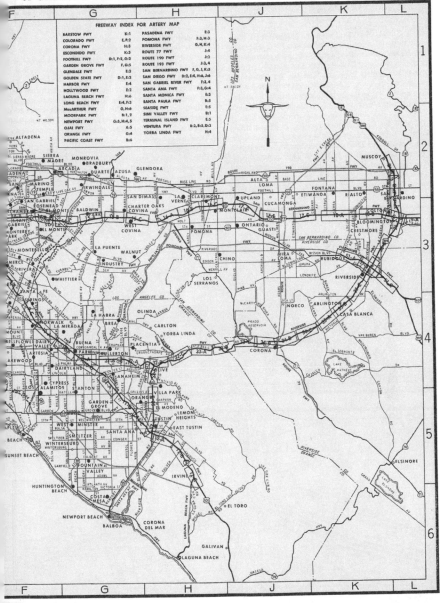

FREEWAY INDEX FOR ARTERY MAP

BARSTOW FWY	K:1	PASADENA FWY	E:3
COLORADO FWY	E,F:2	POMONA FWY	F:3, H:3
CORONA FWY	H:3	RIVERSIDE FWY	G,H,K:4
ESCONDIDO FWY	K:3	ROUTE 77 FWY	J:4
FOOTHILL FWY	D:1, F:2, G:2	ROUTE 190 FWY	J:2
GARDEN GROVE FWY	F,G:5	ROUTE 193 FWY	J:2, 4
GLENDALE FWY	E:2	SAN BERNARDINO FWY	F, G, J, K:3
GOLDEN STATE FWY	D:1, E:2	SAN DIEGO FWY	D:2, E:4, H:6, J:6
HARBOR FWY	E:4	SAN GABRIEL RIVER FWY	F:3, 4
HOLLYWOOD FWY	E:3	SANTA ANA FWY	F:3, G:4
LAGUNA BEACH FWY	H:6	SANTA MONICA FWY	E:3
LONG BEACH FWY	E:4, F:3	SANTA PAULA FWY	B:3
MacARTHUR FWY	G, H:6	SEASIDE FWY	E:5
MOORPARK FWY	B:1, 2	SIMI VALLEY FWY	B:1
NEWPORT FWY	G:5, H:4, 5	TERMINAL ISLAND FWY	E:5
OJAI FWY	A:5	VENTURA FWY	B:2, B:3, D:2
ORANGE FWY	G:4	YORBA LINDA FWY	H:4
PACIFIC COAST FWY	B:6		

PART I

Mother

Laurel Canyon, California

The list of things I thought I knew but did not know grew quickly during my first weeks back in Los Angeles. A hummingbird dropped dead: its wings stopped pounding, gravity took over, its body jumped when it hit the wooden deck. I didn't know that the water in my bird feeder was moldy.

An omen? asks Eli, who is sunning himself in my yard, his tan a mark of leisure, unemployment, and depression. It's 2015 and he's living in San Francisco, his "start-up" circling the drain, his bank accounts depleted by a summer in Mykonos, Spain, Tel Aviv. But here he is, hopping commuter flights to Los Angeles based on his whims or mine, coming home at eight a.m. from an after-after-hours party (*I thought you were at breakfast,* I would say, already at my desk, and he'd laugh in my face before passing out in my bed fully clothed, cigarette smoke wafting up). He slept off entire days, weeks, months of his life. *Oh to be Eli,* was what we said behind his back. It seemed that no triviality of responsibility, debt, or consequence could ever latch on to him.

Is it possible it's a good omen? I ask.

No, says Eli.

I stare at the bird and wonder why it chose me to witness its death. I've always been ashamed of the Southern California mysticism I've kept. But there it is, the belief in a divine pattern just outside my field of vision. It's given me this seeking frame of mind that never resolves or rests but wants to move me closer to a fundamental truth. Mystics, I find, ask *why* before *who what where when how,* a tendency that leaves them bereft of practical knowledge. And this is Los Angeles, a town full of oracles, con men, real estate speculators, all high on self-delusion, self-gratification, marijuana, and a shitload of quartz.

I had just come outside from writing about my father. The writing made me physically tender: flu symptoms would flourish, and I'd sit in the sun until they passed. I moved here in the middle of fire season. A knuckle-cracking wind flies through Laurel Canyon, where I've found a cottage to rent while I wait for my next life to start. Every snap of static is a potential spark.

A few nights earlier I had entertained at the house, built as a hunting cottage back in the 1920s, when the Santa Monica Mountains were filled with populations of mountain lions, deer, and boar, which by the 1920s were well on their way to being killed off, in no small part due to cottages like this one. There were stone stairs carved into the hillside outside my bedroom that led to an old trail. The trail now led to the mansion above me on the hill, whose pool was resting on stilts that touched down near my house. I heard their pool parties. Once a flamingo float was thrown overboard and landed in my yard.

I was still good at dinner parties, a skill left over from my married life, though I was out of practice and now they took me all day to prepare. I swept the dust and debris off the outdoor table in the morning, only to find that by the afternoon it was covered again. The winds. I made a vinegar-braised chicken, an Alice Waters recipe. It came out more elegantly than I expected.

The night was almost too cold for Chenin Blanc, and we wore sweaters. I bought small hurricane lamps at Home Depot, which glowed and bestowed upon this scene a stylishness far beyond my capabilities. The canyon rose up above us, rickety.

I have a friend, someone started, *who was at a party with the fire chief of Los Angeles. He said what scares him most—more than Malibu, or anywhere else in the Santa Monica Mountains—is Laurel Canyon. He said it keeps him up at night.*

We discussed how Laurel Canyon has only one way in and one way out—*single ingress and egress,* is what they call it—which means that not only would the road be swarmed with cars trying to evacuate, it would also be impossible for emergency vehicles to get in. *Not to mention the tiny streets up the hill,* someone else chimed in, *I can barely get my sedan through there.*

All this became clear in the 1950s when the canyon was ravaged by fire and it was impossible to defend. There was the tinder-dry vegetation to contend with, in addition to the density of housing, prolific and vertical, which adds to its vulnerability, as *fire is driven upward when it burns. Cyclonic,* some call those fires. Yet the fires of the 1950s, the 1970s, the early aughts, did not impede building. Quite the opposite. *Look at Malibu.* Real estate companies were given tax breaks to rebuild, homeowners advised to take out insurance, and a cheerful amnesia was prescribed to anyone living near the Santa Monica Mountains, or really anywhere in this disaster-prone city.

The mountains have always been on fire, since Spanish sailors spied this land in the 1500s, calling San Pedro the Bay of Smoke. The Chumash and Tongva Native Americans practiced controlled burns of the hills to avoid the kind of *cyclonic infernos* we have today. These fires seem to be the result of our ceaseless development as well as our failure to fund fire prevention. The prevention itself means there's more chaparral, more sage scrub, more dried-out grasses that light up when the fires and winds do come. And they always come. Yet Californians build, pick through the ashes of their houses, build again. This I understand: *People often act against common sense when they've fallen in love with a fantasy.*

And isn't this Laurel Canyon cottage a fantasy I had? As the landlord toured me through it and I noticed the lack of any updates since the seventies, he said, *Yeah, that's about when Fleetwood Mac lived here.* I signed the check immediately even though I knew I was about to run out of money.

Toward the end of dinner, the winds came like a hot exhale and blew the napkins off the table. Some people made excuses, checked traffic on their phones. The remaining guests voted to move inside. In that foreboding omniscient wind, I felt like a child again.

Why did I come back here?

———

I made up stories from the minute I could speak. A natural escapist, I was always looking for the hidden, real world. I believed—at points—that it existed underwater, or in tide pools. In the roots of trees, or in their branches. In outer space, under beds, in forts of blankets. In the house next door.

I told my elementary school classmates that my father was an astronaut and therefore had to be away from home. I told my younger sister that we were exiled aristocracy, descendants of the Romanovs, and that she must always behave like a princess. I told my kindergarten friends that I was a mermaid—that I snuck out of my house each evening after putting my mother to bed. I ran to the ocean and spent nights racing in the black water with my real family. This is what children do—they investigate reality by contrasting it with fantasy. The problem, as is so often the case, was that I invested authority in the latter, preferring it to the former. Too much unsupervised time and a teeming imagination, too much relentless hope that I could make the invented real.

Children believed me. It took a parent or a teacher to convince my peers I was lying. I remember barreling through people's disbelief with the sheer force of my personality. I refused to relent when caught.

My younger sister, Christina, was and continues to be instinctively loyal to me. When we were little, she corroborated my stories, telling the other kindergarteners that I was indeed a mermaid, even if she didn't quite trust my version of events. I woke up before my sister and my mother and used Crayola markers to color my hair, proof that I had just journeyed from another world. Christina stared at my hair with her mouth open. Many nights she came into my bed and begged me to take her swimming, to make her a mermaid too.

But she couldn't go with me. Not when I dreamed of those night swims, not when I ran away at age ten to go live under the Seal Beach pier, not when I left my house on countless nights to skateboard through empty suburban streets, and not when my mother sent me away to Colorado at sixteen. I don't think my sister saw that it was a gift to be at home, that it was her special power, getting to stay. I think now that I understood exile. I was born a stray.

———

A lot of murders in the canyons, my aunt informs me as we sit down at an outdoor café with good iced tea and niçoise salads. *A lot. Were you alive for that one up on Wonderland? That was the seventies,* I say. She blinks. *No, I was not alive. It was the early eighties, actually. Forgive me, I forget how old you are.*

We order the essential iced teas and niçoise salads. The café is full. People drink rosé. It's two p.m., and no one is going anywhere. The wrinkled insignia of overproductivity, the patina of stress, these people are glistening with the lack of it. It leaves me in a bit of a freefall, of not being pinned down, or knowing how to define my time. A friend living out here said, *It's a different pace. If you accomplish one thing a day—you know, one meeting, one lunch, one workout, just one of those things—then you're good.* I sip my iced tea and watch people accomplishing their one thing.

That was a really dirty job, my aunt continues. *Those people: bludgeoned so badly. And that man, the porn star, oh God, I forgot his real name, how awful, Johnny Wadd though, that was his—ahem—stage name.*

This is my mother's sister, formerly a district attorney of some note. She secured a few convictions in high-profile criminal cases, those successes leading to her being appointed prosecutor to a very publicized murder trial in the nineties. The trial ended with a hung jury. She had a nervous breakdown. She recovered, then retired. She retained her encyclopedic knowledge of crime in Los Angeles, stories that have been told and retold at the dinner tables of my childhood, the city inexhaustible in that respect.

My aunt is disarmingly, harshly honest. She has been since I was a child. She has the posture of a ballerina and had an East Coast education that manifested in that rarest of all qualities: discipline. She taught me the word *atheist* (when I was in kindergarten, at a Catholic school), told me that she wouldn't condescend to me and pretend there was a God. When I was eight, she and I were out to dinner at the Katella Deli. I had an open-faced turkey sandwich in front of me and she said that my father had left us all those years ago because he was a cocaine addict.

What's cocaine? I asked.

Cocaine is a drug. I would lock him up if I could.

It was the same tone in which she had told me, perhaps the same year, perhaps a year later, while we were baking poolside at her house in Palm Desert, that the problem with sex is that it *feels too good and makes you crazy.*

She gave me *Catcher in the Rye* at ten years old. *Justine* by Lawrence Durrell at thirteen. Before she adopted in her forties, she seemed (to me) childless by choice, and deliciously free because of it. She made all her own money and drove a Mercedes, too fast. Obviously, I worshipped her. She was the only adult I knew who didn't drink, which led me to believe early on that she was the only adult I knew.

Yeah, they made a movie out of this murder. Starring Val Kilmer. My aunt dislikes media depictions of crimes that were—to our family—personal. They never got the facts right. The actors were either too pretty or too ugly. *Do you mind if I have some wine?*

You drink at lunch now? Is that considered sophisticated where you live?

I shrug, gesture around me. The line between her eyebrows is disappointed, watchful. She minds. *Never mind, I don't need it.*

Didn't Val Kilmer get fat? Anyway, I knew the DA that tried that case. He came up to me in an elevator once and said, 'I've never lost a case.' I looked at him and said, 'What about Wonderland?' He was a real idiot.

Did you watch that one about Bob Durst?

Watch it? No thank you, I lived it. The police on that one—morons. That was Benedict Canyon.

Stevie Nicks lived in my house, I say defensively. *Or someone from Fleetwood Mac. At least that's what they told me.* How many landlords in the canyon could correctly identify a former New Yorker who cannot resist the allure of that fairy-tale bohemia. That's one LA story. My aunt will not be deterred from hers.

They were all drug addicts, that whole music scene up there. She takes a bite. *A lot of mental illness. It's actually quite sad. And of course, Cielo Drive. Did you know your uncle watched the Manson trials? He was an assistant, still a law student and he sat every day, thinking, what a mess. These people are evil. And they were. Just evil. That was also Benedict, that way.* She gestures west toward Beverly Hills. *Far. But not that far.* She signals the waiter for a refill. *You should invest in some curtains. How's the writing going?*

All these years she's been asking me to move back, and this is the shit she talks about at lunch.

Los Angeles, California

The Monster is what I'm calling the man I love. He loves anonymity, being lost, and privilege, which flying, even with all its misery, undoubtedly affords. The mixture of the three is a state he equates with being free.

I was emulating him when I flew into Los Angeles. The Monster is who I would be if I were a man and had better control over my feelings: loving when I felt like it, ruthlessly irreverent and impolite, ease greasing up all the gears of my life. Maybe I would even learn to love flying.

I was hungover and medicated, coming from what started as a wedding weekend in Mexico and turned into a few weeks of writing and not writing. On this flight there were a thousand things I couldn't say out loud; one was that I was moving back to Los Angeles. I'm only comfortable when I believe I don't live anywhere. But the New York City storage unit constituting my home for the past four years was closed up, the boxes all on a truck, probably stalled on an expressionless highway in the middle of the country.

My things are coming for me, I thought. So was the Monster. I stared out the window, self-satisfied with the dosage of Xanax and box wine I'd landed on. I have a rigorous fear of flying, but on this flight I had a feeling of being too close to something too big to die. The Monster was probably at In-N-Out that very moment, I guessed, planning to surprise me. Thinking I'd be impressed by some generic Southern California thoughtfulness. I would be.

I want a real life, I'd said to him. *I want to unpack these boxes and put things away.* He knew exactly what I meant. Countless times we'd ended it and restarted it. How long had I been in this state of kerosene in the veins, of constant ignition? Casualty of a lust, a rabidity, a purity that burned through all the detritus?

The rest of our lives were the detritus. It didn't matter where I went during this year, and I'd been so many places. He came to me in Brooklyn, in London, in Rome, in Athens. He found me, the way he'd find me in the airport (*don't tell me what time you land, I'll find you*), the way he always found me, intruding on any relative peace I'd scraped together, forcing that joyful explosion every time I returned to him.

So. I'm moving back to Los Angeles and my married boyfriend is picking me up, I thought to myself, smudging the plastic window with my forehead.

Flying into LAX triggered feelings of possession for the endless turquoise-studded grids that reach toward the San Gabriel Mountains. The grid like an outdated network of cells, a massive failure in urban planning, a city built not for humans but for cars. Only a prodigal daughter could see beauty in this sprawl, could look fondly at the yellow banks of smog racked up against the mountains. That daunting Pacific. And there it was, Love for the Monster, for this city, a feeling old-fashioned like salvation, like a narcotic uncoiling. Yes, for us as for so many settlers before us, California would be the golden frontier. Also our homecoming. As the plane descended, I felt dangerously close to healing, a sensation I also refused to recognize as a bad omen.

Laurel Canyon, California

I'm in the middle of a home-improvement project with the cottage, pulling up vomit-green carpet squares and scraping the cottage cheese off the ceilings. The house that Stevie Nicks may-or-may-not-have-lived-in is a mess.

This place is about to fall off the hill, Eli says. *I'm covered in spider bites. The windows don't lock . . . No garbage disposal! Why even leave New York?*

He's right: vinyl flooring coming up warped in the bathroom, mold on the ceilings, raccoon nests under the house, and a sloping foundation that will set a water bottle rolling toward the street. Eli says it makes him seasick. But I'm fixated on improving the floors and ceilings, and to my shock my landlord agreed to renovations. All day my mattress lies on the floor wrapped in plastic and at night I sleep in dust.

My suitcases have erupted onto the floor. Carly comes over and comments on it. *Remember how you never unpacked the entire time we were in Rome?* Carly has a pitiless memory. She's talking about our semester abroad in Rome during college, where I lived out of a tangle of clothes on the floor though an empty closet sat above it.

I guess my eyes are immune, I say to her. I've been traveling for so long I don't consider putting my clothes away. *I'm writing,* I explain to her, as if it makes me exempt. And I am writing. I pitched a national magazine a piece about lost jewelry, thinking it a perfect fit. They asked for alternatives and I mentioned off-handedly that I had something about my father. That's the piece they want, though I said I wasn't ready. *I don't really talk about that stuff,* I said to the editor. But then why did I mention it to a stranger? Because it's coming, unplanned and fevered. With the words come the memories, once dormant, now exposed. They pile up in my sleep. I told the magazine I would try.

It's been two weeks of this writing and I don't leave the house beyond walking to the Laurel Canyon Country Store to buy heads of cabbage or bulbs of fennel. I simmer and smother them with parmesan and butter, then eat it for days. My solitude only feels enterable when Eli tells me he's on the 5:30 p.m. flight to LA. There's a concert and we will be on a list.

You love being on a list, I tell him, stalling.

Like you don't? Come out, come out, wherever you are!

Carly asked me earlier how the writing was going. I responded, *If you find my body first, please turn off the Adele.* Now she calls me: *Go to the concert.*

That's what leads me to my first night out in Los Angeles, where I'm bored. I know I should be dating, meeting people, connecting. I know that my reluctance is considered unhealthy. But as I look around the rooftop of the Fonda Theatre where an after-party has landed, this circle of affluent art-adjacent people feels stifling. In New York, LA, Paris, I see people I've waited on. They don't recognize me, but I know them inside and out: they take comfort in a web of references to restaurants, artists and filmmakers, obscure vacation spots that aren't too obscure since they all seem to be going there, while drinking bottles of natural wine so flawed they taste like kombucha. I see the same faces in Mexico City, Barcelona, Joshua Tree. While I was finishing my first book, living on a tiny Greek island in the off-season, I ran into a New York academic who regularly publishes in *The New York Review of Books*. The world of my adulthood is tiny, and on this evening where, a stranger in my hometown, I asked it to expand, it appears to be shrinking. I've even been to this same Beach House concert before. And the truth nagging at me all evening is this: I'm one of them now.

Except for one tiny thing: I have a love that doesn't rest on platitudes or convenience but thrives on its obstacles. I keep one hand on the phone in my pocket. I think of the Monster, probably at a party like this in his city, weary but looking at the sky. *Whenever I look at the moon*, he says, *I'm talking to you*. I shiver when I know he's thinking of me. We often text each other at the same instant. That won't happen now, because he's with his wife, but I can't stop touching my phone anyway.

The temperature on this night is in the low sixties. I'm introduced to a friend of a close friend, a handsome man wearing a wool cap. I know he's from California. He's not new exactly, but he's refreshing. I see what he's not: rich, entitled, cynical. He's not the Monster.

The Bay, he says when I peg him as a native son.

That's exotic, I say, *I've never been.*

That's not technically true, I go on to tell him. I stopped there once on a road trip when I was in high school. I drove from Boulder, Colorado, to visit a friend attending the University of San Francisco. I arrived in the afternoon. I took a hit of ecstasy at four p.m., spent all night at a warehouse rave in Oakland, then drove down to see my sister in LA, my eyes still rolling back in my head.

So, I do know San Francisco, I joke. *It's very sunny.*

There's nothing more radiant than a woman with a secret. This man sees the heat coming off me but has no idea of its source. Is he simply a visual creature, he likes the way I look? I don't know why men are charmed by this shit. But they mostly are, a performance of derision and confidence, abrasive edges smoothed out with self-deprecation that hints at vulnerability. I don't know why they love that I'm divorced, why a thousand red flags don't shoot off in their brains when I tell them—eventually—that I've cheated on everyone I've ever been with. I don't say it with pride. It's shame and honesty. A warning. I never say, *It will be different,* but I must shimmer with promises. I'm doing it now, it feels like I'm yawning, stretching up out of a confined space, my hand unclasping my phone, coming out of my pocket, I gesture, I pull my hair back behind my ears. The man smiles at me, and there is a loose thread in that smile I want to tug; his eyes look like he wants to play. He turns to introduce me to his girlfriend and I, also, smile.

———

There was a story my mother told me about her childhood, an afternoon with her father, my grandfather, back in the sixties. They had parked on the bluffs of the South Bay and were walking down a trail to picnic. Down beach, something caught my mother's eye. The cliffs of Palos Verdes are continuously disintegrating. The Portuguese Bend, miles of coastline on the edge of the peninsula, remains undeveloped only because it's too geologically unstable to build upon. As you drive the long, pock-marked and tar-scarred coastal road in the evenings, you can see it: the road particulating, waves evaporating as they crash below the bluffs, the ice plants and coastal sage leaning off their ledges. Elsewhere in Palos Verdes there are Mediterranean-style mansions, manicured gardens, roads winding into the hills where horses stand at attention in oak fields. But what I remember is the dark pull of this coastline, relatively isolated in the middle of Los Angeles.

A car flew from the cliff, as if on cue, as if a prop, and sailed down in an arc, whistling, until it crashed nose-first into the ocean. My mother and grandfather stayed as the police arrived, but he took her home before the driver was fished out of the water. The man was, *certainly*, my grandfather assured her, *DOA*.

Why did he do that? I was a child asking her. I already thought the area was haunted. My sister and I were often left with my grandparents in Palos Verdes on weekends. Sometimes we stayed weeks. Every time I saw a car parked, admiring the view, I felt that vertiginous pull.

The driver had had enough, she said.

Enough of what? I wondered but didn't ask.

I remember this story when I wake up in Laurel Canyon with a view of an empty hillside where there was once a house. It sailed down in the rains, *all the way down Laurel Canyon Boulevard,* my aunt says.

They've cemented the hillside to prevent further erosion. Around the cement, greens have come, unexpectedly. It's been a wet autumn. Neon-green grasses, moonlight aloes with orange and yellow blossoms. Cacti exploding with green stretch marks. Every morning the same lunatic chores: I wake up, every day, to texts from the Monster. He is sometimes in my time zone, more often not. He has texting hours, as most married men do, but I do not. I am always open, available, flexible.

When they are relevant, he tells me about his dreams: *Last night we were driving, there were redwoods. You were talking in the front seat next to me, but I couldn't hear you.* I don't know if this is supposed to make me feel better about our situation. He thinks I should take comfort in the fact that he never forgets me.

I check the weather in New York City. I test out some statements about myself to start the day: I wrote a novel and it will be published. I stopped waiting tables. I can afford to live by myself (something, at thirty-one, I've never done). The Monster and I are in love. *I'm in love!* I try to say to myself. I can never deliver that exclamation point. I'm not twenty anymore.

It's in the forties back in New York, a day when the drizzle and gray won't lift. I seem to have survived some test the city gave me, though I do not feel victorious or even that clever. What I've purchased, with the working till four a.m., back at it again at nine a.m., the debt, the divorce, the minute and massive sacrifices, is not the book, but an absurd freedom. No mortgage, no marriage, nowhere to clock in and tie on an apron. I have my friends on both coasts, my sister, Polaroid photos from countless sparkling parties, meals so decadent and rarified they were unrepeatable. I also have the potential for *more*. This should be the happiest time of my life.

I tell myself this each morning. But the truth is that I'm stalked by this exposed feeling of failure. A belief that being here is admitting defeat, that the ground is too unsteady to walk on, the air too dry to breathe. I think my aunt is right, I should put curtains up. But then I wouldn't see the coyote that comes and eats the cat food I leave out for the stray cat. The coyote is so close to me while he eats that he sometimes bumps his nose into the glass not five inches from my face. I watch him, not blinking, not knowing that the stray is another thing that by feeding I am close to killing. Every morning I refill the dish with cat food, encouraging prey toward predator, conflating care with threat.

I rinse the coffee cup, a tannic brown residue left from yesterday. I clean things and they become dirty again. In New York I never had the kind of life that created small clusters of dirty dishes. I could use every plate in the house for entertaining. And I created garbage, with iced coffee cups and take-out containers. But I worked odd hours, ate at least twice a day at whatever restaurant employed me. I feel new to the rhythms of inhabiting a home.

Now every morning the kettle, the blooming grinds, the hum of traffic on Laurel Canyon Boulevard, the squirrels stealing pomelos from the tree. While I drink coffee, I stare at a map from the *Thomas Guide* I have tacked up on the wall. It's the *Thomas Guide* I used to study in the back seat of my grandparents' Cadillac. I can see the pastel-pink south peninsula, the bourgeois Palos Verdes my mother came from, the blue-collar San Pedro my father came from. All of it seeming to be important, though I feel nothing.

What about your parents? the guy from the concert asks, holding a coffee cup and toast. A few weeks ago we spent the night together and he made me laugh the next morning. I purposely didn't take down his phone number or his last name (*Look at you!* my sister texted), but when a text arrived from him a day later, I was—to my own surprise—relieved.

Now I make breakfast for him occasionally. Nothing too elaborate. He's in an open relationship with the *girlfriend* I met at the Fonda Theatre—his use of the term makes me laugh out loud, but I don't ask for further explanation. I'm not available, even if I wanted to be. He's curious about me, seems fueled by a restless curiosity in general. He's a landscape architect who knows more about my birth city than I do. The way he inspects the cottage, you can tell he loves to fix things. *He's not your type,* Eli says dryly after that night at the Fonda. That comment is meant to be mean and reductive, like this guy is nice and I'm not. Accordingly, I roll my eyes when I talk about him.

Not close, is all I say to him about my parents. That's what I've always said, from the minute I got away from them. That's not so surprising, is it? If he presses, I'll say my mother lives down the 405 freeway in Long Beach. I'll say I don't know where my father lives, but I believe him to be in Washington. If he's surprised that I don't know where my father lives, I'll shrug. *Like I said, not close.*

This has worked for me for a decade. People I've worked side by side with for years, whose weddings I've attended, whose heartbreak I've nursed, know nothing about where I come from. I arrived in New York City from school in Ohio, and I wanted to start over. *Tabula rasa.* That's something I miss about my restaurant friends: they didn't ask why I never went home for the holidays, only cared if I could pick up their shift. I miss that shared understanding of evasion.

But you're from Los Angeles? the Love Interest clarifies. Yes, he's the Love Interest. He's shirtless and barefoot. He has been digging in my garden—though I never asked him or invited him to, he's there all the same. Every time he leaves, I assume it will be the last time, but then he's back and I'm only sometimes annoyed. He smells like health but cleans the dirt out from under his fingernails before he touches me. All the windows are open, and he's looking over the map with me. I point to Laurel Canyon, then to the south peninsula.

Not really. I wouldn't know how to get from here to there if you paid me.

Long Beach, California

The children who stayed at day care until dark had stories to tell, but not the voices to tell them. It was a Catholic school, so divorces weren't as common as the national statistics of the 1980s reported, and those of us coming from "broken homes" were acutely aware of how different we were. Most of the other moms didn't work. The staff handled all of us who stayed until dinnertime gently.

A car door would slam, and I would lose focus on whatever I was drawing or painting or gluing, my entire body a satellite searching for her high heels on the asphalt. She would appear in the doorway, nothing like the other moms with their smudged faces, skewed ponytails, sweats, minivans, packed lunch sets. Her legs shimmered in her nylons, which she shed like snakeskin when we landed back home. She hemmed her skirts an extra inch, *because I'm short but my legs are long,* she informed me. Those legs appeared, then the rest of her, in silk skirts, blazers, camisoles or button-down blouses. Then the eyes, bright (*my eyes,* she would say while considering my own), and her youth, wafting off her like Chanel No. 5. She never looked tired to me, but I can see it now, how her posture had wilted by day's end, how she still had to feed us, bathe us, read to us, sing to us, sleep with us. She never intended on being a single mother of two by the time she was twenty-nine, or a barely glorified secretary to a judge, clerking her way through a thoughtless, uninspired forty-hour workweek. But when she arrived at day care in her professional regalia, other left-behind children stared at her, jealous.

I already knew she was fragile. I don't know many single mothers who are able to hide their pain from their children. There isn't enough space. Crying while she balanced the checkbook. Panic attacks while driving us. Crying on the phone with her mother, berating our absent father on his answering machine. One night she fell chasing him out of the house. She twisted her ankle. He didn't come back. She sat on the lawn crying and my sister and I ran to her. I remember my fear. I remember exactly how she tried to get back up quickly. How she gripped her ankle and sat down on the lawn, defeated, curling into herself to weep. Shortly thereafter I went through a phase where I practiced calling 911, hanging up when I heard the passive voice.

When my mother and aunt asked me to explain my actions, I said, *When you don't have a father, and you have a baby sister, you have to be in charge when your mom falls down.*

After your dad left, you wouldn't let her go to the mailbox alone, my aunt remembers. It's gross and total, the way I can feel the tug of my love for her. My protectiveness. Her skirt hems, her Chanel purses, the cigarettes and hairspray. Clutching at her, shrieking for her if she disappeared for even a moment, running to her when she came into any room, done pretending that I was strong, independent, or cared about anything else. I know what it's like to be claimed by the most beautiful woman in the world. She was mine.

———

My father told me they met as undergraduates at the foreign kids table during lunch at Loyola Marymount University. My mother was fluent in French and Italian, my father fluent in nothing. I can't quite piece together what they were both doing at that specific table. Were they loners? Were they trying to escape the South Bay where they grew up?

There is, unfortunately, another likelier story. My aunt says they met at my mother's boyfriend's apartment in Manhattan Beach. My mother's boyfriend being a very well-established coke dealer in Los Angeles in the seventies. *The last I heard of that boyfriend,* my aunt recalls, *he was serving a twenty-year sentence.* The apartment—I imagine—had views of the ocean. Mirrored surfaces that made cocaine shine. A terrace where my mother could smoke and stare at the horizon, which is what—I imagine—she's doing that day when my father comes out for some air. Tall, dark, and handsome. The two of them brushed powder from their noses, ran tongues over gums, introduced themselves, chattered in a fast-forwarded, intimate way.

What did you love about him? I asked my mother when I was a teenager, wondering if I had missed some central story that would make their animosity toward each other logical. Beyond a transaction related to one of his visitations, I never saw them spend more than five minutes in a room together.

He was handsome, she said, edged. *He didn't age well.*

That's it? Really?

My mother sighed. *He gave me you girls. Isn't that enough?*

What did you love about her? I asked my father. That was when we were living together, and I had gotten to know him some-what, how intolerant he could be of women. I couldn't imagine him being able to stand her.

I was young, he said, and cleared his throat. *I remember there was a lot of pressure.*

That's not an answer about her.

She was a good mother.

Was she?

When you were little, he says.

My parents locked me out of whatever feeling provoked them to choose each other. Their passion and pillow talk and how they imagined their future. Things I hope exist or else the entire enter-prise is too sad.

I used to scour photographs of them for clues, wanting them to make sense beyond the well-mannered expectations of mar-riage. They traveled together. My mother studied in Rome, my father at Oxford (where—he once told me when he was fucked up—he had gotten a girl pregnant and he had to *skedaddle* when she wouldn't get an abortion). Here are my parents in Paris, Milan, London, rural Italy, visiting our relatives, sipping cups of grappa. Here is my mother on her honeymoon in Santa Barbara, her blond hair dyed dark, looking Italianate finally, standing next to the plaque with her new last name hung on their cabin. She's tan and smug.

I did that for your father, she said when I showed her the pho-tograph. *He loved my hair dark. The minute I kicked him out I went back to blond.*

This was when Christina and I were teenagers and she took us to Rome. Her voice was softer, more voluptuous, because we were traveling. We were about to tour the Pantheon when my mother paused and pointed up to a hotel. It was a *pensione* on a noisy street. The front had potted flowers gone brown and twisted in winter.

When I lived here, I was in a dorm, but when your father came to visit me we stayed in this hotel. It was very adult, and fifteen lira a night. One time I wanted to surprise him, make my hair dark. I bought a box of dye at the drugstore, but apparently didn't let it set completely. We got into the bath and it started to run, turned the water brown. I was so embarrassed. Then it came out all over the sheets.

That's all I know. They stayed in cheap European hotels. She loved him enough to dye her blond hair brown. They took baths together and her hair leaked. They stained sheets.

Long Beach, California

It's always ten degrees cooler down here, my aunt is fond of saying when I arrive in her corner of Los Angeles, stunned by the weather. *That's why the taxes are so outrageous.* She lives in Naples, a cluster of three tiny islands surrounded by Venetian canals in Alamitos Bay. It was designed in the early twentieth century, marketed as a "Dreamland of Southern California." The water in the canals is disgusting. But gondolas and crooning gondoliers make their way through the waterways, and people stroll with glasses of wine in the evening, tend to roses with gardening gloves. *You should come over and take the kayak out.*

But I'm not visiting my aunt today. I haven't been in a kayaking mood lately. Instead I'm sitting in the car my grandfather loaned me—he's ninety and could still drive it if he wanted to, he just doesn't want to—parked on my mother's street in Belmont Shore, a bit away from the canals and their grace.

I'm looking at my eyes (*her eyes*) in the rearview mirror. I wonder how I fell back into this so quickly. I've let my defenses down, no potential advantage to be won by this vulnerability. Being on her street in the middle of the day is unmistakably a mistake.

In the rearview mirror, I've accidentally aged from girl to woman, my looks overleveraged by the amount I've depended on them to protect me. Every line in my face, every sunspot is a reminder of what I have to pay back. I am the age she was when she picked us up from day care. Every mirror or window brings me back to her, to the way she used to look. Here we are.

People tell me stories about their own narcissistic or kooky mothers and then sigh, *But you only have one mother.* I've thought about that a lot in the years I've been gone. That she is my one mother, mine to call monthly, or mine to ignore. During those years I sometimes thought there might be space for more. That hurting each other cannot be the sum total of what we mean to each other. Maybe I can start something with her now that I'm back. Be the kind of daughter who visits her mother once a week. I can take her to movies or to the nail salon. It will be like a friendship. Or something.

Or I could leave. Of course, I could leave.

I am thirty-one years old.

Ten years since my mother had a brain aneurysm that left her mentally and physically handicapped.

Four years since she started living with a (technically homeless) man she met at Alcoholics Anonymous, and less than a year since her last sojourn in rehab.

Sixteen years since I stopped living under her roof, after our relationship became abusive and unsustainable. Sixteen years since she sent me to live with my father, who was for all intents and purposes a stranger. Sixteen years since I told her that if she sent me away, I would never come back. That turned out not to be true, as I moved home in 2005, after her aneurysm, to be her nurse for a summer.

I hope you didn't move home to make peace with your mother. You don't owe her anything, my aunt says often, *after what she did to you.* While I appreciate the sentiment, I always find the statement oddly and willfully blind. My aunt is forgetting, or ignoring, my bid to live with her when my mother and I fell apart. How I begged not to be sent to my father in Colorado. How I tried to be good when they had me over. I babysat my cousin, who was then a little girl, in a bid to prove my virtuous influence. Does my aunt really not remember when she said *No?*

Occasionally, if we've spent enough time together and she's softened, I think she remembers it. She'll put the words into her husband's mouth: *Gary says his greatest regret is turning you away.* That approximates her own regret, without her having to own it. *Your mother wouldn't allow it. And your grandmother forbade it. It was your grandmother.* Again, this all strikes me as curious—my aunt has never really taken orders from anyone. I think that my aunt was afraid of me. I know now that a family is a delicate equilibrium. I wasn't so delicate at sixteen. And in the contest between believing her sister, and believing her adolescent niece, she chose her sister. That seems fair to me.

But still she feels the need to absolve me from the imagined guilt I must carry from being away for so long. My aunt is skilled at making the world into black-and-white. She has an old-world flair for absolutes, which made her a great lawyer. Right and wrong. Debt and credit. My mother deserves punishment, I do not owe her forgiveness, etc.

I tell myself that what I owe my mother and what she owes me stopped mattering a long time ago. In order to want something from her, I would have to believe she was still my mother.

When anyone asks, my sister and I say our mother's short-term memory is gone, but it's not exactly true. If I arrive and ask her what she ate for breakfast, she can tell me (*coffee,* she would say, suspicious, always a defensive woman, even before, as she says, *I got a hole in my head*). If I asked her the last time we spoke, or how long ago her aneurysm was, I'd get a sloppy guess (*Last week? A few months ago? Four years ago?*). Her long-term memory is selectively intact, depending on the day, but one gets the feeling that she uses it for whatever slim advantage she can garner. She remembers the name of the street she lived on in Rome when she studied abroad in college (*Via Lattanzio* near the Vatican) but doesn't remember, she claims, the turbulence of my adolescence.

It takes her a long time to assimilate new information, especially if presented from afar and inconsistently. Our few phone conversations haven't been full of questions, but statements that my mother tests out. In person now it's the same. She adds a hesitation at the end and waits to see how her audience responds. I do a lot of nodding, but I do more correcting.

You're married, she begins.

I'm not.

You're not married to Brad.

I am not married to Brad anymore.

You live in New York.

I do not. Anymore.

Your sister lives in New York.

She does.

You live in . . . she stares at me, straining, *. . . Brooklyn.*

I did live in Brooklyn. I live here now, kind of.

Kind of.

I'm trying it out.

You live in Long Beach.

I live in LA. In Laurel Canyon.

You live with . . .

I live alone.

This loop will repeat itself at least once before I leave. To be fair to her, I didn't tell her about my divorce for a while. There is never any rush to give her information, because I spend years confirming and revising her statements. The same thing happened when I got married in the first place, a year of repetition over the phone—but at least in that instance the news was good. She could clap her hands together and walk away from the phone feeling proud of herself. This news was distasteful. Her brows knit in frustration trying to remember what happened to me, though it is beyond her to simply ask.

You work at the wine store.

No, I wrote a book. It'll come out next year.

Oh, that's right, that's right. You're a writer.

A pause.

And now you're . . .

Writing. Another book.

Oh. I see.

She does not, in fact, "see." There is no recognition that my writing a book is an extraordinary occurrence. No memory of graduate school, the accomplishments, scholarships, sacrifice it took to afford said school. No surprise I'm being published, nor recognition that I've essentially won the motherfucking lottery. It's the same to her as if I still worked at the wine store I started at when I was twenty-three.

I'm quite numb in this house in which I have no memories, this tiny house we moved her to when we realized that there was no money or hope of money. To visit with her, I make myself microscopic. I'm hidden away in a recess of my body (my shoulder, my rib) and I don't think things that will hurt me. I'm a charming blank, and if I can stay that way, I'll drive away from her in one piece. I do this because I imagine that I bring some variation to her colorless days. Or that she feels my absence as a punishment, and I don't want to punish her. I guess I imagine, sometimes, that she loves me. And that being around a beloved is universally agreed upon as beneficial. Right? I don't know.

I can't look directly at her. Her physical devolution in the years I've been gone makes me heartsick. I end up looking at her things: the porcelain spaniel figurines on the mantel, her cookbooks, the sun-faded spines of my childhood, British histories and art histories and Shakespeare, everything tattered as if water and wind had wrecked the house, a tangible storm mirroring the psychic storms made of white wine and rage. Her teakettle dented and caked in dust. There's a small bedside dresser in the living room with a locked top drawer, the key of which was always hidden in different spots around the house. Inside was her jewelry. She doesn't wear it anymore, but I'm reminded that all the women in my family are absurdly attached to our rings.

I don't look at how frail she is. Her clothes—picked up at Ross or Loehmann's, ill-fitting and off-colored to begin with—won't stay on her shoulders or hips. The skin on her arms hangs translucently off her. I don't look at the bruises from where she's fallen, or the way her dyed hair has grown out, half of it black and gray and then a strong line where the bottom turns brittle and blond (*if I encountered her on the street, I would cross the street,* my aunt says). I don't look at her browning teeth, the gums receded from years of smoking, the front tooth knocked sideways from falling while drinking, or at the right side of her face which has sloped so that one corner of her mouth is frowning, the implications of that slope something I cannot handle, and I don't look at her eyes (*my eyes*) which have sunk into the crepe-crinkled, sunspotted skin of an ancient woman (I see other sixty-year-old women, parents of friends, and my mother looks like she could be their mother), and I definitely, definitely do not inhale, because between her breath, her unwashed, weepy-eyed, obese dog, the cloying, cleaning-product-laced ammonia scent of alcoholics and shut-ins, all I can smell, if I were to allow myself to, is death.

But what hurts the most—if I had feelings anymore, which I assure you, I do not—is not remembering her from my childhood, or even before the aneurysm, when she had a flattering amount of Botox and worked out enough to comfortably wear a bikini at forty-six (*my legs are long*). It's that after the aneurysm, it appeared that she would get better. That summer of 2005 when I moved in with her to nurse her. I would hold her hand and repeat what the doctors had said: *You're a miracle.* And that is always what I'm hoping for, isn't it, something akin to a miracle? Instead of a dulled impasse, wherein I want things to be different, and am distraught because they can't be.

She's staring out the window, silent. I look back at the books. There's nothing awkward between us now. No pressure to say anything, to entertain each other, to arrive at any intimacy. It's a conversation with no structure beyond our script and no momentum beyond manners. She's huddled into a corner on the couch and hasn't moved since I arrived. She can't get up, I realize. I had let myself in. I had leaned down to hug her. Her boyfriend—who takes care of the house, lives off her small savings, and keeps her up to her eyeballs in booze—placed her there before he left. He will return when he sees that my car is no longer parked on the street.

I realize that I wanted to go on a walk with her. Maybe that was the reason I drove down here in the middle of the week. That

writing about my father, thinking about the two of them, is hurting me, and a walk with my mother would prove that time can
mend hurts. I'll ask her to get up, ask her to sit in the backyard.
I'll get her walker. She'll make an excuse for why she wants to
remain on the couch. I won't accept that excuse. She'll refuse me.
I'll have caught her and then what? If I push, she'll do what my
sister and I call *play brain-dead*. She's doing it now, disappearing
at will, suddenly deaf, blind, mute. I know in my bones that she
hasn't left this house for a long, long time. *I don't owe her anything,*
I remind myself. She breaks the silence.

You have a boyfriend.

Kind of.

Well that's good. It's good to have a boyfriend.

I want to laugh, but I nod.

Los Angeles, California

I'm ashamed to tell Carly.

Our lives have diverged so drastically that we're nearly the clichéd opposite of each other. I know this is a facet of adult friendship. The fact that my choices appear more and more regressive is harder to swallow. For a moment in our mid-twenties, it seemed like we were headed in the same direction: she was opening a cold-pressed juice store, I was helping to open restaurants, she had her first child at twenty-six, I was married the same year. We would text from bed on opposite coasts and marvel at people who were still living like . . . well . . . like they were in their twenties. As if our choices had aged us a decade beyond our peers. We traded recipes, sent each other vacation rentals in Big Sur or the Cape. We would jump on the phone to talk about how long to soak the salt cod for brandade.

I shattered all that self-assured placidity three years ago when I told her I was leaving my husband. That I was in love with an artist (I stand by that, but he was also a bartender). I didn't care about anything: our obvious incompatibility, his lack of money, my own lack of money, or the annihilation of what was a very nice life. It took her the length of a phone conversation to compute it. She asked if I could see myself with the artist long-term. *Not really*, I said. She asked if my husband had done something to earn this decision—was he mean, did he cheat, did he drink too much? *He does drink too much, but he's not mean. He just loves me.*

What do you want? she asked. *When you imagine your life in five years, what do you want it to look like?*

When I called her that time, I was sitting on the floor of my apartment in Williamsburg, alone, taking in all of my belongings but feeling no relation or possession. I had already disappeared from that life.

I have no idea, I said. *I just want more.*

She sighed. *That's a hard way to live.*

Once Carly figured out that I was self-destructing with no plan, nerves frayed by lust, she was concerned. *You guys need therapy. Or better yet, have a baby. You won't have time to get into trouble like this.*

I'm not in trouble, I said hotly. *I'm in love.*

She was quiet on the phone.

Now, I've been traveling alone for most of the year (my affair with the artist long ago flamed out as it was always certain to), and Carly is postpartum with her second child. She lives in a house in Santa Monica, with furniture and framed art, a backyard with a play structure, her husband. Her mother-in-law in the guesthouse. Her juice company is thriving, they add locations monthly. She goes to the Santa Monica farmers market every Wednesday.

In between these travels, I lived with my other best friend, Alex (Carly, Alex, and I went to Kenyon College in Ohio together and have been bonded to each other since), at the house on Devoe Street in Brooklyn. Alex kept the third bedroom for a closet. We costumed ourselves and ate rare steak every night.

We knew people who could get us in places. Or I was with Eli at a basement dance party enmeshed in dazzling boys who shoved poppers under my nose (*Are you being safe?* Carly used to text me while I was in Cairo, in Mykonos, in Palermo. *LOL,* I texted back). But the majority of nights, I ate dinner alone. I read constantly (*I don't understand having that kind of time,* she said) and I booked plane tickets in my sleep (*When are you coming home?* she wrote me. *Tell me where that is and I'll come tomorrow,* I said).

Carly and I know we are lucky to connect, despite envy, confusion, and sometimes a lack of common language. There is a respect that isn't a given after fifteen years of friendship but is earned.

Maybe that's why I avoided telling her about the Monster as long as possible. Alex, my sister, Eli, they all knew. They had met him when it started. But still I didn't tell Carly. I avoided telling her until I was so fucked up with hurt and anxiety that I needed her.

I've told her it was over more times than it's actually been over. The last time I told her, I could see that her patience was thinning: *You're in a relationship with a married man. He's going to go on vacation with his wife. That's what married people do.*

The time before that I called her, enraged, after Eli ran into the Monster and his wife on the street in the Mission. (*Yes,* said Carly, *that's what married people do, they walk on the street together.*) More time has passed and now I have to tell her, *Surprise! It's not over.* I have to listen to myself say, *This time it's different,* because I do in fact believe it's different, while in the foreground her son builds fortresses out of Magna-Tiles and her daughter has learned to pull up on the coffee table. Her husband, Alejandro, used to make pozole when I crashed on their couch, or would take us all down to the beach at sunset. He usually leaves the room when I bring the affair up. I see him just barely shaking his head when he thinks he's out of view. I've become their wayward teenage daughter. I can't remember when I was an adult like them.

Today I brought a lawn sprinkler with me, so their son, Luca, and I can run through it in the overbaked autumnal heat. Being in Carly's home is like being held: things are white and made out of linen or alpaca wool or marble. They burn the expensive incense. I barely clear my throat before she says, *Please don't say what I think you're about to say.*

———

My great-grandmother's ring, the snake ring, is passed down to the eldest daughter in each generation, which it is my fate, my great privilege, to be. My family talks a lot about inheritance. That means money, jewelry, real estate. Sometimes we mean recipes, silver, linens. The inheritance of the snake ring is something else entirely.

My great-grandmother Adelaide was married and divorced three times. She made fortunes and lost them, abandoned her children, and was "married" a fourth time in a ceremony at her nursing home to one of the few men left alive. It was so they could sleep in the same bed. Somewhere along the line, Adelaide took all of the diamonds from her wedding and engagement rings and turned them into a new ring. A snake.

It's a phallic symbol, my aunt said to me. The ring had been hers, the eldest girl of her generation.

It sounds cursed, I said. I was eighteen years old.

She dropped it into my hand. *The curse isn't the marriages. It's Adelaide's sex drive.*

San Francisco, California

Of course, it's not true that I've never been to San Francisco. Even that basement rave when I was seventeen is not the whole truth. San Francisco is the Monster's home. I was visiting Eli in that city when he invited me on a walk. He had seen my photo in the paper. I had sold my novel. *I always knew I'd see you on the other side,* he wrote me. He means that we grew up together in Seal Beach. He then wrote, *Congrats,* and with a pleasant condescension, *I'm not impressed you wrote a book. I'm impressed you started a business with no capital. I doubt you know anyone who's done that.*

It's hard to remember the innocence we possessed, so hard that I begin to doubt if we had any at all.

What is true is that I've never been to San Francisco on a gray day. It's always brilliantly blue, hills suspended in water, so that the hills seem to be drifting. I'm constantly disoriented. I asked no questions about where we would be walking. When I arrived, he said, *You're going to walk in those shoes?*

I was wearing sandals. I looked at the Golden Gate Bridge ahead of us. *Wait, where are we going?*

We were never friends. Later we would say that even when we

were kids, we must have known that there was the hum of a third rail between us. A quickening when we saw each other. He dated girls I knew, and I would confide that they weren't good enough for him. I lost track of him when I moved to Colorado. Then came a fortuitous meeting when he walked into the restaurant where I worked in New York City. That became the occasional Facebook message or email—we were still protected by geography. This kind of crush is built on ideas of someone, their perfection enhanced by ignorance so that we could point to the other and say to ourselves from a safe distance, *that's the kind of person I could be with.*

I hadn't seen him since he completed his PhD in engineering. He was recruited to be the senior vice president of a music streaming company—a vague position that allowed him to travel constantly (*sounds like a bullshit job,* I said sweetly).

I'm addicted, he admitted. *The weird in-between places, the arrivals, the departures, the lounges. The strangers.*

I asked about his wife, whom I didn't know. They married right out of college. He told me that marrying her was the smartest thing he ever did, and I believed him. I felt that way about my ex-husband. People like us fasten ourselves onto those we think are safe. I told him how I was haunted by my divorce. By how big my promises were, and how few I was able to keep. How being a young wife made me feel unfit and destructive, and that a lasting marriage really comes down to how you both behave in a crisis. My ex-husband and I behaved badly. I told the Monster that I was still—three years later—recovering.

I have so much more respect for it now, I said. *It's really sacred.* I meant marriage.

He considered that.

The vibrating tenor of this conversation is as old as adultery itself. The high of prohibition, the stepping in and out of ambiguous, flirtatious conversation. Is it revolutionary that we both loved to read? That when we argued it felt like foreplay? That our minds felt faster and sharper in the spark of the other's? That we were physical immediately, pinching, slapping, bumping into each other?

It wasn't his intelligence or stories: the one about losing his virginity to his mother's friend—*on a family vacation, no less*—or how he was kidnapped during a surf trip near Tijuana and his friends pitched in two hundred dollars and a Nokia cell phone to get him released, or how he was on a tiny plane that ran off the runway in Japan. I did love his perversity and how global he'd made himself. But that's enough for dinner, not enough to risk my life over.

It was when he told me how embarrassed he'd been by his father's clothes when he was a teenager. I remembered his father riding a bike through Seal Beach and giving money to the homeless crew near the pier. When the Monster talked about times he had almost died. Talked about getting his heart broken in college. Talked about quitting drugs when his best friend overdosed on heroin.

In middle school I'd watched him bodysurf from the pier, but he was just another lost boy in the water, tips of his hair blond from the sun. Now he listed the bridge's suicides as we walked. He had shed all his boyishness. When he said he was sometimes unsure about his marriage, I understood. *I get it,* was all I said.

After talking about himself for some time, he suddenly asked if I remembered seeing him during the summer of 2005 when I was in Seal Beach, nursing my mom.

You used to walk your mom on the block. On a leash. I would see you from my bike. I waved one time, but I didn't know if you saw me.

I stopped walking.

When I was teaching Nancy how to walk again, she had a big Velcro harness and a leash. Sometimes she would cry at the door because she was embarrassed. I'd put a baseball cap over her head where the hair was growing back and help her get sunglasses on. I said, *We'll hide from the paparazzi.* I would take her out of our house and tell her we were going to make it to the ocean, three blocks away. We only ever got to the end of our block.

How could he have seen that vulnerable moment? Caught me in that state of care that I never let myself think about, let alone talk about? There was suddenly something bigger between us—history. When he said that, he entered me directly, bypassed every brick wall I've put up to other men.

Because I'd stopped walking, he stopped, and was turned toward me. We were still on the ascent on the bridge, I could smell my own sweat, my sunglasses slipping down my face. My sandals by the end of the day would give me bloody blisters. When we were still, there was wind I hadn't noticed, and that feeling of drift came to me, as if we were moving away from the known world. We had been hiding, side by side, so we didn't have to look each other in the eye. We stood about six inches apart and I thought, *We are fucked.*

I did walk her, I told him. *I didn't see you.*

Do you also remember, he asked—and I had this feeling that he was just warming up, that he had something in store for me that wasn't this walk, or the picnic he'd packed, or this city on the sea, but something ambitious that would unfold over the rest of our years—*when you ate the pizza off the ground?*

I laughed. I did remember it. I must have been fourteen. A group of teenagers on Main Street, terrible pizza by the slice. *But you weren't there, were you?*

I was there, don't be rude. You were wearing a yellow sundress and riding that pathetic longboard you used to skate. You had no shoes. Your feet were black on the bottom, it was fucking disgusting.

He continued: *You dropped your pizza and it fell cheese-side-down onto the sidewalk. You looked so sad and I said, You can still eat it. And what did you do?*

I thought, *I can trust him, he's smarter than me. He won't get us into trouble.*

I picked up the pizza and I ate it, I said, trying to control my smile.

He nodded. *You picked up that filthy piece of pizza and you ate it. You were a monster. And that's when I knew.*

Knew what, I should have asked, but didn't have to. We walked until the sun set, while sailboats toggled beneath us like toys in a bathtub. I knew too.

Long Beach, California

*I*magine *an inner tube,* my mother's surgeon said. *Imagine a bulge appears, where the rubber is weak. Imagine putting pressure on that inner tube, the bulge growing. Can you imagine what I'm saying?*

It was March of 2005 and we were in Long Beach Memorial Medical Center. I had flown in from Europe, where I had been studying abroad in Rome.

Your mother won't live, my aunt said when I got ahold of her. I didn't have a cell phone, so she didn't know how to find me. She called my school in Rome but I was visiting Max, my first love, in Madrid. It's evidence of how distant I was from my family that when my aunt finally called Max's mother, she was able to get in touch with me immediately.

I called my aunt back from a phone booth. It was Good Friday in Spain. Every shop was closed, row after row of steel grates over storefronts, and all I could think was, *It's finally happening.* The specter of tragedy stalking my family had arrived.

An aneurysm is a bulge in an artery in the brain. A bulge can appear and go unnoticed because it has no symptoms. What happened here is a rupture.

What happened here is a rupture.

When an aneurysm ruptures, it floods the brain with blood, an event technically called a subarachnoid hemorrhage, commonly called a bleeding stroke. They are most often fatal. Sixty percent of the people who suffer them and survive live on with brain damage.

My aunt over the phone: *You better hurry up.*

When my sister and I arrived in Long Beach, we were told our mother would never come out of the coma she was in.

The surgeon: *It can be random. It can be caused by high blood pressure. Sometimes smoking increases the chances that it ruptures.*

She smoked, I said. *A lot. And drank. Like an alcoholic drinks.*

He already knew. *Like* an alcoholic? The doctor's folded hands. Where were the adults? Was I really alone, at twenty years old, in his office as I remember it? Did I invent him to console myself?

There's no time of day in the ICU. I was hollowed out and sedate from the Klonopins I bought from a classmate back in Rome. I bought them for fun, not necessity. Max flew with me, breaking up pills and ordering Heinekens, feeding me pretzels when I woke up from sleep gasping *It's not real,* in the business-class seats his parents upgraded us to. Max must have been in the waiting room while I talked to the doctor. Christina must have been somewhere—was she sleeping? Or was she making conversation over tepid coffee and vending-machine Cheetos with all my mother's ex-husbands and ex-boyfriends? Even my father flew in.

It can also be hereditary, the surgeon said.

The drinking or the aneurysm? I asked. Genuinely.

I watched men walk all over her. When we were little, Christina and I were expected to entertain her boyfriends, to convince them to stay with her and by extension, us. We put on concerts, choreographed dances. Spent extra time choosing our outfits, fixing our hair before they came over. In a few instances we asked them to be our new father. There were more men than was prudent. Some of them treated her appallingly. One night I heard her and a boyfriend in the backyard, outside my bedroom window, fighting. He was calling her *a stupid bitch* in a soft, terrifying voice. I went outside in my pajamas. *Get out of our house*, I said to him. I wasn't ten yet. *We don't need you.* My mother was so drunk she could barely talk. She sent me back to my room. I was wrong. She did need him. They continued dating.

By the time I was in high school I was used to watching my mother drink herself into semi-consciousness at the kitchen barstools of our house in Seal Beach, then try to master the staircase. She would paw at the wall instead of using the banister. This was our big house, not the shitty, trashed rental we had to move into whenever she and her current boyfriend broke up. Richard was a charming but shallow lawyer who kept a safe in the garage filled with cash and guns. He didn't believe in banks. He was always kind to Christina and me. He bought us the big house when he and my mother got back together. After many years of fighting, he finally married her.

We were lucky to live there, and we all knew it. The time at the rental had been tense, eight hundred square feet filled with outbursts, my sister holding pillows over her ears while my mother and I screamed. We blamed the confines of the apartment, but even in the bigger house, not three blocks from the ocean, there wasn't enough air for my mother and me.

At that point, it had been years since she asked the barest questions about my life: who my friends were, what I cared about, who I wanted to be. I was failing classes, constantly in detention, and when the report cards came home, she only raised her eyebrows at them, proof she was right about me. I would come home stoned and instead of running up to my room, I would stalk her in the kitchen, begging for confrontation. I would stand at the fridge eating chicken salad with my hands, opening bags of tortilla chips, microwaving Hot Pockets I bought myself at the 7-Eleven. I was either hiding from her rage or trying to get her attention—there was no safe middle ground while she was drinking. I stared at her while she looked, fixedly, at the small television.

Leave me alone, she slurred.

Why can't you be happy? I asked.

Leave me alone, she said again. She pretended to file her nails. *Go to your room.*

I sat on the countertop and ate with a stoner's abandon, totally invisible to her. When she saw me again, she was startled. She said, point-blank, *Some people aren't meant to be happy.*

What people, I wondered but didn't ask. *Me?*

That's bullshit, I said. *You're just lazy.*

You're lazy. She said this half-heartedly. This happened, that she got too drunk to hold on to an argument. *And you're selfish. Just like—*

—My father. I know.

I continued eating, my hunger bottomless. I opened cupboards, ransacked bags of chips. She continued to watch TV.

Some evenings she would sketch while she was drinking. When I was a child, in a fit of optimism she had taken interior design classes at a night school. Another such mood had her looking at real estate in Santa Fe (*I can actually breathe there,* she confided to me, turning pages of a *Sunset* magazine). A door would open up in her and through it I could see our escape. But her enthusiasm over projects, trips, and potential lives was terribly short-lived. If I tried to bring it up again, she silenced me quickly. It came down to money. The muddy secret of our life was that we never had any money. As a court clerk, my mother didn't make much of her own. My father's child support was inconsistent at best. My grandparents bought her first house. They gave us an allowance, paid for private school, bought our clothes, took us on vacation. My mother's second husband bought her the next house. *They control me,* she would whisper, her teeth purpled from wine. *They use the money to control me.* Every dream died on her and left a bitter stain.

Still, she would occasionally take out some graph paper and start sketching a new house for us. Maybe she would leave him, she would say, sell the house. Move to Hawaii. *Yes,* I would say when I was little. *Let's go together. Why not?*

It's not in the cards for me, she said.

What cards? I wondered. I wonder still.

———

They all had blue eyes and loved to drink. Adelaide, my great-grandmother and snake ring creator, was a genius and a lunatic, my grandfather told me. One of her favorite party tricks was to run out of the house after dinner, screaming, and hide. She would come back in the morning, dress covered in dirt, laughing. One time she found an ax in the shed in the yard and used it to break in the front door.

An ax?!

My grandfather holds his hands up like he's not to blame. I

Mother · 49

remember her and her petite brown cigarettes from the nursing home. In her late eighties she still had a drawer full of lingerie.

Adelaide's daughter, Peggy, my grandmother, was also a genius and lunatic. She had a photographic memory. Though she had no college degree, starting with only a few thousand dollars she played the stock market until my sister and I had enough money for college. She absorbed numbers and the roving Dow in her sleep. To bed she wore seafoam-green silk nightgowns and a headset she connected to a tiny television. The ticker tape rolled over her barely closed eyelids, rinsed in blue light. Each morning her eyes were as glassy and straight as a gambler's.

She was a magnificent drinker: tumblers of scotch in daylight, bottles hidden in bookshelves, inside unused soup tureens. By sundown she talked to herself and to ghosts. She looked right through me, even if I was curled up against her. As the hours waned, she called out, "Mama, Mama." I realize now she was calling for her own mother, not mine.

One night she stumbled up to adjust the chime on the grandfather clock. She was a theatrical stumbler, falling while soft-shoeing in a dim room, falling at parties, falling while trying to stand up from the roulette table on a cruise she took us on. My aunt is still wounded remembering her first wedding reception, where my grandmother got so plastered she fell in the middle of a conversation with Tom Bradley, the mayor of Los Angeles. But I watched as she fell that night. She pulled on the innards of the grandfather clock, the chains and pendulums, and it fell with her, tackled her, and pinned her to the floor. She broke a rib and took to her bed for a week.

Later it strikes me as heartbreaking that my grandmother was looking for her mother. When she was seventeen, her mother fell in love with a sea captain and headed to Vegas for a quick divorce.

Adelaide left her daughter, Peggy, in the care of friends. It took me a long time to see that was abandonment. It helps explain her anger, her fast hands that could hit you before you had time to flinch. It helps explain why she encouraged my mother to send me to Colorado and forbade my aunt from taking me in.

The last time I saw her we took a borrowed boat for an early evening cruise on the Naples canals. My grandfather motored us into the bay, passing students rowing crew, children being packed up from waveless beaches. The boating was an activity she hated, and the subtext was that she was doing it for me. She was preparing for a hysterectomy as part of her treatment for colon cancer. I was leaving for Colorado in two days, and we barely spoke. She died a month later.

It doesn't occur to me until I'm back walking those canals to visit my grandfather, that my grandmother and I have an adolescent abandonment in common. Did she plan it that way? I have told countless people that the move to Colorado was *the best thing that ever happened to me*. I am sure that my grandmother said the same thing about her own mother leaving her. I am sure we both said that it made us stronger. That it didn't hurt because nothing my mother did could hurt me anymore.

I really believed that until I moved back here.

Long Beach, California

My grandfather's house is right on the canals. The thick green water rises, recedes, breathes, outside his windows. He and my grandmother moved from Palos Verdes right before I started high school, and here, my aunt says, *Grandma was so miserable she died.* I wasn't planning on seeing my grandfather, but I need to restore some harmony broken by my visit with my mother.

He's napping on the couch and his nurse, Gilda, is in the middle of a puzzle. The house is stuffy and a television plays Fox News, muted. I wander up to my grandmother's room while I wait. She died fifteen years ago, and her room remains untouched: the staggering armoire dusted, bed made, mirrors polished. The effect is more impersonal than haunting (there are no trinkets, no photographs), as if the cleaning lady had just come. My aunt and I call it *the mausoleum,* not least because it's covered in royal-blue *toile de Jouy* wallpaper depicting pastoral idylls. Her room looks over water, but the shutters are always drawn. I crack them and sit in a large upholstered chair—it is also covered in *toile* but in linen. Remarkably, it smells like her.

The *toile,* this fusty, British room in this coastal landscape, is laughable. But it is a perfect emblem of the WASP world she tried to maintain. There were the stories: ties to the Daughters of the American Revolution (loose at best); our "cousin" Clara Barton, Union nurse during the Civil War (affiliation also loose at best); her childhood rivalry, auditioning against Elizabeth Taylor in Hollywood (which, though my grandmother was beautiful, seems a stretch). There was her lifestyle, where her values shone. My aunt and mother were debutantes, went to private schools, rode horses, traveled to Europe. They sewed curtains and did needlepoint, took lessons in dance, voice, and French (my grandmother cringed when I started taking Spanish in middle school). But more than that, they were educated in a kind of domesticity that boggles my mind, groomed from the time they were little girls for marriage and motherhood.

My grandfather was the dirt-poor son of a newly arrived Italian immigrant, a towering, abusive man. My grandfather was one of six, and mostly raised by his sisters. As he explains it, every immigrant wanted to marry a native WASP. That was his American dream. He still says marrying my grandmother was the smartest thing he ever did. She had *social skills*, she was like *taking the elevator to the top floor*. She was *the love of his life*.

This is both true and untrue. My grandparents used to make the walls shake yelling at each other. In my lifetime they never slept in the same room, or even the same wing of the house. And for all my grandmother's social skills, the rigorousness of her manners and decorum, the bridge-playing and piano lessons, her drinking is her defining characteristic.

Look who it is, Granddaddy says. He's standing in the doorway. *It's nice to see you in this room.*

He doesn't age for me. He was an old man when I was born

and is the same old man now. I tell myself that means he will never die. *Have you ever considered new wallpaper?*

He nods, as if he's turned off his hearing aids. It's impossible for me to see my grandfather unsentimentally, though I'm now an adult and can see that the stories don't add up.

James Vercelli Ferrero III served in the United States Navy for three wars. He was one of the small team of men who developed, built, and journeyed on the USS *Albacore* submarine (at the time, 1953, the most advanced research submarine on earth), and he went on to be an engineer at Howard Hughes, where he shook hands with *the great man* himself exactly three times. He personifies the postwar aerospace boom that developed (some would argue, destroyed) Southern California. And he is correct that he rocketed straight through the expanding middle class to the ranks of the upper when he married my grandmother and installed his family in Palos Verdes Estates. But his politics are hard for me. He can be cold. He was once also a drunk, before he turned jaundiced from a weekend golf bender in Pismo Beach and his doctor made him cut back.

And yet, when I look at him, as I am now, watching him inspect the wallpaper lightly, the way he blinks away his emotions when he notices that I'm wearing my grandmother's earrings, I see a hero. A man apart from time, not for what he did for his country (which I admire, but in all honesty cannot possibly understand), but for what he did for me and my sister. He was the only male figure in our life, and he and my grandmother partly raised us.

He's the only thing that stood between you and a double-wide, my aunt says. She's not wrong. And yet, this is only one aspect of a man whom my grandmother accused of having a secret second family, who was—by all accounts—a terrible father and husband. *Who knew he was meant to be a grandfather?* my mother and aunt would say, ruefully, watching him dote on us, sitting rapturously through our every Christmas concert and ballet recital.

I was visiting Nancy, I say to him, explaining my presence. He approves of me visiting my mother. Daughters visit their mothers, that's the final, orderly word on that.

I'm a little disturbed, I say. *By what I saw over there. When was the last time you saw her?*

She doesn't want me to visit.

Did she say that? I don't think she knows what she wants.

Is her boyfriend still there?

I nod.

It's a bad scene, he says.

He shakes his head, pained. I follow him downstairs where he inquires after his car (*You don't park it on the street, do you?*), my financial situation (*Still making a living basket-weaving?*), and obliquely about my love life (*You have anyone to take care of you?*). He apologizes for not having money anymore, though I haven't asked him for a cent after he had to finance my last year of college out of pocket. The money has dried up and he doesn't know how to relate to me without it. The fact that I've been able to quit waiting tables can't assuage the anxiety he feels about the precariousness of my path, or his embarrassment that I had—at thirty-one years old—been waiting tables at all. Every decision I've made troubles him. My apparent ability to survive fascinates and irks him. I'm proof he doesn't know the world anymore.

Do you ever think about the future?

I'm just not sure what that looks like, I say.

He is desperate for tasks: maintaining his car that he doesn't drive, filing my mother's tax return, making my aunt run "death drills" where she comes over and he watches her open up his computer, find the documents, open the safe. Or being the permanent mailing address my driver's license is attached to. Though I don't care about the junk mail he's collecting, or his inspection of his car that I'm borrowing, I like that he thinks it's holding us all together.

I'm not sleeping, he tells me, while Gilda puts together a turkey sandwich for him. *I wake up. I can't go back to sleep.* He's genuinely perplexed by this disobedience. The Navy taught him to sleep anywhere. And to put ketchup on his scrambled eggs, causing my grandmother to sigh: *Once a pleb, forever a pleb.*

That's pretty good, I say, regarding his sleep. *All things considered.*

All things considered. Since everyone else is dead, that's pretty good?

He's aghast that he's old. Lonely since everyone has died. Planning obsessively for a future that he knows, rationally, is more and more limited by the day. Unfortunately, at ninety, there's nothing wrong with him. Aches and pains, but he's mobile. Jarringly alert. He just got an iPhone. He calls my sister and me to troubleshoot it. But today it seems somehow unjust, actually frightening, that five minutes away my mother seems to be in a semi-coherent state of decay, immobile in front of a television that plays and replays *Casablanca,* while her father just learned how to send photo messages of the sunsets.

Has my mother seen a doctor? I ask, directly. *Does she go to AA meetings? Has she left the house? Can she shower herself? Can she walk? How does she eat? It looks like she's had some sort of stroke—*

He puts his hands up for me to stop.

—and she's covered in bruises.

He shakes his head. In a voice that reminds me of my grandmother I say, *Now, don't cry. Just tell me what's going on here.*

Cut it out, Gilda says to me sharply, dropping off the sandwich. She's only twenty years younger than my grandfather but she's strong and ageless. She was Audrey Hepburn's nurse in the last years of her life. She once won the lottery. She's from the British West Indies and my grandfather is so enamored of her he tells me—weekly—that if I want to write a book, I should talk to Gilda, because that's a real story. He's right.

Sorry, Gilda, I say automatically.

My grandfather doesn't touch his plate.

It's too hard, honey, he says. *I don't have it in me. I'm old.*

I put my hand on top of his hand. I feel betrayed. Why did I think he was in charge? Because he collects my mail? Again, that voice of my grandmother's, cruel and uncompromising: *Because it was easier those years in New York to believe someone else was taking care.*

Joshua Tree, California

The Love Interest takes me camping in Joshua Tree, one of his treasured places. It's a place of spiritual significance to so many, invoking the park borders on sentimental. He is a sentimental man. He's bent on making me fall in love with California again, or perhaps he thinks I'll fall in love with him.

All across the horizon I see the dark silhouettes of people climbing to the tops of the pockmarked, orbital boulders, the prickling shadow of its trees. We've scaled our boulder with blankets and jars of wine. Our campsite laid out like a playground below us. We've turned west for the sunset. I think I hate these parts of California away from the coast, the dust, the ache of dryness, but then I've never inhabited them like this.

Can I tell you, I never once thought the desert beautiful until today, I say to him.

Those are desert eyes. When I first get here, all I can see is the brown. Then after a day or two, I get my eyes and the nuances come. The faded colors, wildlife, all the flora.

Desert eyes, I say, pocketing the phrase. *That's good. I'm keeping it.*

Even when you're in a place like this?

What?

You're always writing?

No, I say, lying. *There's nothing to write about Joshua Tree. It's beautiful. No conflict.*

You can't write if there isn't conflict? he asks. He thinks he's teasing me, but it's a real question.

Two people went camping and drank wine while the sun set? I ask in return. *It was one of the most peaceful landscapes she had ever seen?*

He is a man who calls his parents once a week to catch up. They have been married for thirty-six years, together since they were sixteen. He tells them real, true things about his life, asks them for advice. He believes in achieving a state of happiness and believes in sex as one way to get there. I remember when my couples therapist told my ex-husband and me that we were bonded by damage from our childhoods. The Monster and I were bonded by the same shared ache, this feeling of *not enough*, unworthiness that kept us in a constant suspension of trust. I can't explain my past to the Love Interest without admitting that his wholeness feels juvenile to me. Perhaps it's a defense mechanism, but I don't think I can outgrow it. As I gaze with him at the gaudy lavenders and oranges of the sunset, I think of how proud I've been of my independence. When this man talks about his parents, I realize that I haven't had another choice. On these evenings with the Love Interest, I feel ancient, and also stupid for not believing anything can bond people besides trauma.

He's telling me about a study on soothing landscapes, about a tableau of fields, a river, yellow rolling hills, and a road going through it. There's a tree in the foreground, which promises shelter, there's water, the promise of life, the yellow hills imply wheat, promising sustenance, and the road, a journey. People from thirty-one different cultures pointed at this as the most beautiful image.

All those promises, I say. *It sounds like something you'd see in a doctor's office. I don't know if I've ever been attracted to that kind of landscape.*

No, I wouldn't think so. A woman in love with conflict.

Seal Beach, California

My mother didn't hit me often when I was a child. A slap here or there, something she learned from my grandmother, who used to smash my head into the wall if I misbehaved. But my mother couldn't stomach spanking us. She took so many hits from my grandmother, she knew if she started lashing out like that, she would not be able to stop.

She stopped caring when her drinking got worse, which it did with her second marriage. I look back for a sign, a trigger, something to explain why she stopped caring what kind of parent she was to me. If there was something, it remains hidden to me. I used to ask Christina why our mom hated me, but she was too naïve to guess. She said, *Maybe because you don't put your stuff away?* My grandmother said I was too much like my father. *That's impossible,* I replied. I didn't even know him.

My mother waited until we were physical equals—until I was as tall as her, weighed more than her, when we had already been at each other's throats for years—to start trying to physically dominate me. It started with breaking plates to make her point. Then one night she threw a Pyrex glass at me. It bounced off the wall and didn't shatter. Then the hitting, hair yanking. Christina ran up the stairs when it started, she'd hear a tone of voice and she'd be gone. She'd lock her bedroom door.

In our family we use Mason Pearson brushes, an extravagance that started with my great-grandmother Adelaide and has made its way to me—there's one lying by the sink in Laurel Canyon. Occasionally when I pick it up, I remember the back of that smoothly sculpted plastic brush against my cheek when my mother smacked me with it. Hard enough that it would swell the next day. A rupture. She kept hitting me. I curled into myself, shielding my face, and the brush cracked against my skull, then my neck and back. She had never hit me *with* something before. I remember thinking, *Where are the adults? Someone has to stop this.*

Another rupture when I pushed my mother. I don't remember understanding how close we were to the stairs, but I do remember suspecting—I was *on fire* with the suspicion—that I was stronger than her. The stairs, her stumble, the wine, the wine, the wine. Her tiny frame in that large nightgown, parachuting while she tumbled. I immediately heard my grandmother's voice indicting me: *She pushed her mother down the stairs.*

I ran down after her. The fall wasn't impressive though it was the whole flight. What was impressive was that after years of this same fighting—slaps taken and returned, the cursing, the door-slamming, the horrific shit we said to each other—I was shocked, no I was *terrified,* that I was as strong as I thought. Once I had tipped the power balance, I was at sea, sinking with regret.

You're okay, I said, binding her hands so she couldn't hit me, trying to comfort her. *You're okay.* I watched her register, in that underwater, sodden way, that she was at the bottom of the stairs. *Just get up,* I said firmly.

I got her into bed and wanted nothing more than for her to be in control again. It was far, far too late. I was already partially living with my best friend, Taja, whose family had a generous habit of taking in strays. I was already failing out of high school. My grandparents stepped in, negotiated. My mother and I saw the therapist we had been with for years. We tried again. A month later she kicked me out and changed the locks.

She threw my clothes away in big black trash bags. Christina called me to retrieve them before they were picked up. I rode my skateboard up to the house from the alley. My sister watched from the upstairs bathroom while I poked into trash bags. I waved at her. *I'm OK.* I skated away with one bag sitting on the front of the board, another on my back, wearing the pajamas I had slept in the night before at Taja's house. I rode to Walt's Wharf, the seafood restaurant where I was employed as a hostess. I clocked in. I have always found solace in work, real mind-blunting labor. I found my work clothes in the trash bags, the white button-down horribly wrinkled. I found my clogs. *It's fine. I'm free,* I told a concerned coworker. I was never going to be controlled. I was never going to be dependent on anyone. Was that it? The first moment I knew I could burn a bridge and survive? That my survival became colored by spite?

That fall down the stairs was really the end of any pretense of my mother and me being able to live together. Adults I knew worried about me, offered to feed and house me. Even my teachers heard about it. I lived with my best friend for the next two months. I'm not sure what my mother told her friends, about who or what instigated our separation. Sometimes she would call the police on me and say I was a runaway. They would show up to claim me. *She's an alcoholic,* I would say to them. *She kicked me out. I'm not safe there.* I had an older boyfriend who helped me take steps toward an emancipation. I went to a few Al-Anon meetings with senior girls who were already on the verge of getting sober. I was sixteen.

After that night we attacked each other, we stopped speaking for a long time. We never spent more than a few days under the same roof until she was released from the hospital and I moved in to be her nurse for the summer.

————

First, we were told she would never wake up. Then, if she did, she would never speak or walk. Then three weeks later her eyes opened. Blink, blink, blink. That's all my mother did. She blinked, at the strangers around her, plastic tubes filling up her throat. We talked in careful, soothing voices and touched her hands. We thought we were connecting, as if she knew us.

Did she, in fact, want to be touched? How horrific to be handled by anyone and have no recourse. How condescending, to not know where you are or who you are, and everyone in the room cooing at you like you're an infant. Sometimes her blinks were pained, panicked.

My aunt: *She was technically dead. They weren't even going to operate. Your grandfather stopped a surgeon in the halls who was leaving—his shift was over—and begged him to come back. He stood there weeping and said, Save my baby.* It's here my aunt sighs. *I wouldn't have done it.*

————

The night of my mother's aneurysm she was at the gym. She had turned forty-seven one week earlier and was going through a renaissance with her body. She was keeping herself "bikini ready." She was engaged to her boyfriend, Bruce. He would be her third husband. They met on eharmony.com. They were shopping for rings and had a trip to Hawaii planned for the next month.

She was working out with a trainer. I've asked many times what exercise she was doing. The gym won't tell me. Treadmill? Weights? Just stretching? I believe she complained of a headache. She remembers a headache. And then she hit the ground.

I do not remember my aunt or my grandfather escorting me to her room at the hospital. I remember the nurse, Jamaican. She sang hymns to my mother's unconscious body day and night.

I remember Christina and me in the hallway of the ICU, and greens, the color of illness. We're drenched in green light, and various adults are trying to prepare us. I ask my sister if she wants me to go in first and she shakes her head. We hold hands. As we walk down the hallway, I look into every window of every room, trying to meet the eyes of every patient.

I think now it's a blessing that our loved ones are often so unrecognizable. No one looks like themselves in the hospital. The veil of illness has come over them. The woman they said was my mother had a face ballooned from the blood. Wrinkleless, her cheeks like an ironed sheet. Her head shaved, a line of staples curving over the left side of her skull. A puzzle forced back together. Her body sunken into the bed, silicone breasts floating on the surface. She still had flecks of dried blood in her ears.

Bleeding out of the ears is bad, my aunt said firmly. *It means brain damage if she lives.*

What undid me was my mother's tongue, bloated and protruding, suppressed by the tubes of machines making her breathe.

Her tongue like a dog's, like a child mimicking disgust. Or exhaustion.

She's just a little girl, I whispered into my sister's ear. It was my first thought. *Look.* I tried to turn her toward our mother, who I reasoned was not really our mother. I think I was saying that she wasn't responsible any longer. That she was our child now, that we mustn't think of her as a mother. *It's okay, she's just a little girl.*

I remember the smell of my sister's hair when I held her face hard to my neck. I remember being grateful that she has always smelled the same. (When they first handed her to me, covered in brown fur, sullen, wrinkled, red, I was twenty-one months old and said to the adults, *My baby.*)

But I can't remember noise. None from Christina or the machines keeping Nancy technically alive. I remember thinking if my sister cried it wasn't my turn to cry, that we would have to cry one at a time.

I left my sister with my aunt in the waiting room. I excused myself to the restroom, shut the door, locked it. I looked at my own eyes, my mother's eyes, my grandmother's eyes, my great-grandmother's eyes, and I said, over and over, *She's just a little girl.*

———

Long Beach Memorial hospital was proud of my mother. After three weeks in a coma, she opened her eyes. They removed her throat tubes—scratching, then scarring her vocal cords—and she gnawed on syllables. Groans. Yelps. More time passed and she spoke. Nonsense at first, lovely infantile gibberish. She still relied mostly on blinks: one for yes, two for no. On the cover of their newsletter, the hospital published a photo of her sitting in a wheelchair in their community garden. She's collapsed into one side of the chair, like an infant that can't hold its own weight yet. She was considered *a miracle recovery.*

My grandfather and aunt were desperate to buy time, to buy more physical therapy, more medical attention. There were too many unknowns (Would she speak? Would she walk? Would she be able to work again? Drive? How would we afford twenty-four-hour care?). We read that the first three months were crucial in determining the success of recovery. My aunt got us two additional months at the hospital, and during that time, hope seethed through us. The right side of her body was initially completely paralyzed, but after a month of daily acupuncture and physical therapy, she could do small steps with a walker. She would be coming home.

I was supposed to be in New York City that summer, where I had been every summer and winter break since college started. I lived with my boyfriend Max's family on the Upper East Side, a generous and warm family where everyone, even his seven-year-old sister, was intellectually inclined. We often danced in the living room after dinner. Max's mother was my best friend—we went to yoga together, gossiped for hours. I was somewhat undomesticated after years with my father—I didn't get haircuts or buy clothes. She took me to her salon. Bought me a Lilly Pulitzer dress. We regularly got manicures together. We all went to their house in Vermont for weeks in August and swam in a lake. While friends took unpaid internships at theaters and PR companies, I unpacked boxes at the Borders in Columbus Circle. I wore a back brace while breaking down pallets and did overnight shifts counting inventory, and I still felt privileged because I was close to books. I was so infatuated with the city, the archaic East Coast and its customs, that I sometimes cried when I drove in over the bridges. Seal Beach was claustrophobic and dismal by comparison.

But my sister begged me to come home. My grandfather demanded I come home. There was talk of my not being able to finish college because of expenses. Everything was on hold until we saw what we were dealing with. *Your mother needs you,* my grandfather said. There would be no New York. I had missed so many classes in Rome that my teachers didn't know how to grade me. I took my finals, then flew back to Los Angeles. *A miracle recovery.*

We didn't have money for full-time care, but two days a week we had a professional nurse, Luz, from the Philippines. She was a little lax with my mother, but she was kind. Five days a week I was the nurse, with my sister helping when she could, although this became another thing I imagined I was protecting her from. I often wonder what would have become of my mother if that care ratio was reversed. Or if Christina had been in charge. I know that I tried.

My mother was the size of a hummingbird. The hospital escort carried her up the stairs to the master bedroom, carried her in his arms like a little girl. She didn't remember her house—those wide frightened eyes, her pulse racing so that I could see it flickering on her wrists. She didn't speak a word that first day.

Home is where the miracles started shrinking. Her fiancé, Bruce, who was present at the hospital every day for months, visited less and less. Then his calls shrank as well. Each one left her confused and agitated as she tried to connect to him and remember him. After one phone call, in which my mother mostly mumbled and nodded, I asked to speak to him.

I need you to stop calling.

He cried into the phone. It felt obligatory. He was spineless, the kind who can't be around other people's pain without revealing their own weakness. I had only met him once.

It's just . . . I have a son . . . I'm not rich . . . I can't . . .

Bruce, I said, through my teeth, *of course you can't. No one is blaming you. Grow up and stop calling her. She'll forget in a week.*

He continued crying. Eventually I hung up on him. Yet for all my bravado, very few things gut me as thoroughly as the memory of her saying in the bathtub, in that squeaky, doll voice, *I have a boyfriend, right?*

She had to ask for her memories back from me. When I recall the times I've had steel in my blood, where I wanted nothing but to survive, it's my grandmother's voice that comes out in me. I felt nothing looking at my mother, though her face was falling. *No. You don't.*

Her brain will make new connections, Dr. Chan had assured me. In the beginning she had no memory at all, no recall even of her daughters. But slowly the long-term storage unpacked itself. We didn't know if the short term would ever quite arrive. It was over a month before she knew her own name, or what time of year it was. He gave me instructions on how to nurse her. We had exercises, physical and mental, daily. I read books on brain trauma. Biweekly acupuncture appointments. She had a weekly meeting at the hospital where she sat with the other survivors and they tried to talk but mostly just sat together, their aliveness its own success story. I bought flash cards for different age levels, games, crossword puzzles, coloring books and colored pencils.

She was okay with basic emotions. *Happy,* she read off a card. *That's right. Do you remember a time you were happy?* A tree or a flower, structures of civilization. *Do you know the names of any trees? What happens when the light turns red?* She could identify a hospital. An airplane. A family.

I don't want to do this, she said, and considered her hands in her lap.

I know. I put the flash cards down. *Me neither.*

A dream of mine from that time of a parade on a country road: pastoral New England, a dirt road and cattle fences beside it. The parade is more like a caravan, everyone wrapped in tunics. Some wrapped their faces and I knew they were God. There is a broken section of fence. Through that break, which I know is the break in my mother's brain, each person throws a trinket, an offering. Lockets, bread, dolls, scarves. I am standing aside holding tools, anxious for the parade to finish so that I can get back to repairing the fence.

It's there in the dream: my small reserves of patience, waiting for an apology, a recognition of the pain she caused me, an idiotic, child's amount of hope that she would care what happened to her.

At night, I listened to my mother's fluttery, hummingbird breaths and felt the force of how quickly lives change. Not just hers, but mine. Wiping out her memory had wiped out my entire child-hood. I had Christina, but she was younger than me. Our ver-sions of events vary wildly. It felt like there was no witness to my growing up, no one paying attention anymore, as if the backdrop had fallen away revealing an empty soundstage. The aneurysm also took away our chance to fix anything between us. It was all gone.

Eventually my sister and I slept together in another room with a baby monitor. That first week I slept on a cot in my mother's room, sometimes right outside the door if I couldn't handle it anymore. "It" wasn't the gross stuff. I didn't care about taking her to the toilet. Cleaning out the staples in her skull. I didn't care about showering her, trying to shave her legs, trying to tweeze the hairs around her nipples which had grown long and wavy at the hospital. Didn't care about helping her with tampons when her period surprised us. Didn't care about brushing her teeth, icing bruises that welled up every time she hit a wall.

It was her breathing while sleeping. Panting while dreaming. I knew in her dreams she didn't know what happened to her. She would wake up confused all over again. *Where am I? And who?* When I watched her sleep, I understood that to love is neither exhilaration nor safety, but instead this: painful, too tender, forc-ing a forgetting that's close to forgiveness.

Long Beach, California

When I arrive to take my mother to her first doctor's appointment in at least five years, her boyfriend, Larry, is home. He opens the door already crying, on the offensive. I plummet into the surreal, repetitive reality of drug addicts and the mentally ill. It's a place I can navigate, which is why I don't immediately get back into my car or call the police.

Please, he begs me, his morning tremors in full effect as he grabs my arm, *you have to take her.*

My mother is sitting on the couch with her arms crossed, mouth set. *I'm not going.*

Get your walker, Nancy. I had been calling her by her first name when I felt I had to be firm with her since I was thirteen.

She can't walk, Larry says.

I can walk, she says, contentiously. *But I'm not going to.*

I use my smoothest voice: *Why don't we try, Mama?*

It takes both of us, Larry on one side, me on the other, to pull her to standing. She's yelling at us the entire time, scratching along the walls of the house, her legs shaking. I see how weak her muscles are, how her limbs buckle at the slightest pressure. At the doorjamb she starts crying. Her nose is running over her face and into her mouth, her hands are flapping, *I can't do it, I can't breathe.* That's when I lift her. She calls to Larry for help but holds still. I carry her against my body, rigid, across the lawn and into the street. I put her down outside my car and say, *Put yourself inside, I know you can do it.*

It takes ten minutes, but she does it, dragging her partially paralyzed right foot into the car with two hands. I shut the door and turn to face her boyfriend, whose terror of me is palpable. When I really look at him, I notice how gaunt he is. Something wrong with his pancreas, I'm remembering. I really don't know which one of them is in worse shape.

You should have called me, I say to Larry, using my manager's tone, in which I used to admonish servers for being late. My mother watches us angrily from inside the car, like a dog who has been banished. He turns away from her, still crying, trying to hold on to me, a stream of bullshit splattering out of his mouth:

He tries, but he can't live like this, he can't keep her secrets anymore, God how he's suffering. His children tell him to leave my mother but he just can't, he loves her too gosh-darn much, chivalry isn't dead. But my mother hasn't left the house in years, she made him stop going to meetings, she drinks two bottles of wine a day, she forces him to drink, he tries to stop her but she wakes up after he's asleep and she walks to the liquor store to buy her booze.

It's here that I stop him, that I decide this farce cannot go on.

Larry. You're telling me that that woman—I point to my mother through the car window—*that woman WALKS to the liquor store by herself—in the middle of the night—and buys booze?*

He holds on to both my shoulders. *Every night. I can't stop her.*

And yet it goes on. I grab his shoulders back and speak slowly, gently. *You are lying. I'm taking her to the doctor now.*

My mother and I are silent on the drive. I'm texting my sister, not just at stoplights, but texting constantly, needing her with me: *Emergency, emergency, this is bad.* My mother plays brain-dead, looking out the car window, not a tear left on her face.

When we arrive, she won't get out of the car. She holds on to her seat belt. When I try to unbuckle her, she hits me, then gasps like I might hit her back. I leave her and go into the office to check in. There's Dr. Chan. I saw him quite often when I was the nurse ten years ago. The relief I feel at seeing him, the adult reality of him, makes me feel temporarily safe. This might be okay.

Where's your mom?

She won't get out of the car. My voice cracks a little. I want him to hug me. I want to abdicate all responsibility and lie down on the floor. I swallow it. *It's a bad scene. Do you have a wheelchair?*

I sit in the wheelchair across from the open passenger seat in a mostly empty parking lot. A gray coastal day, fog that would burn off by noon. We are—as I should have expected—an hour late to an appointment that is a ten-minute drive from her house. I told her that we will not be leaving until she sees Dr. Chan. We're sitting in a sort of stalemate. I'm really just catching my breath.

She picks at her cuticles and I stare at the mute, office-park architecture, wondering if there are normal people inside doing their jobs. What do those jobs look like? Email marked *urgent*, new boxes of pens and paper clips. All of that life unrecognizable to me in the one I'm living.

I'm not going in there, she says eventually.

I know, because you're drunk, and you don't want him to know, I say.

What I want to say is, *How could you do this to me?* The answer is, she can't help it. Not because of her brain, I'm realizing today, but because this is who she always was. This is who she was when she was too drunk to pick up my sister and me from friends' houses in the evenings, or when my sister came home and found her unconscious in a puddle of blood from falling, and who she was when I was thirteen and we fought and I screamed at her to *stop*, to *please stop the car*, I couldn't breathe, if she didn't stop the car I would throw myself out of it. She yanked a fistful of my hair and said, stone cold, *You think you're special? You think you're the only one who wants to die?*

Additionally, this shell of a woman in a Long Beach parking lot is still the little girl I saw in the coma. When she doesn't respond about her state of insobriety, which is an affirmative answer, I find I'm crying. Not enthusiastically, like she was, snotting and yelping while we got her out of the house, and not like Larry's histrionic weeping. It's the resigned, accidental crying of a child who knows no one is coming. I don't look at my mother. I try, I really do, to keep myself tiny, silent, and numb. But I feel it coming and then it has arrived, my hurt: it is massive, I can't see beyond it.

Here are your options, Nancy. You go in to see your old friend Dr. Chan. Or I drive you to detox at the county hospital, not the fancy fucking place in Newport Beach you usually go. As you know, detox sucks, and I won't let them give you Valium. While you're in detox, I'm going to get a lawyer. I have lots of money now, I'll get a fancy lawyer. When you get out of detox, I'm going to put you in a nursing home, where you're the only person not in a fucking diaper, and they won't let you drink, and you won't be able to hurt yourself. I look at her. *And you will never see me again. I swear to God, Nancy, I will not think twice about it.*

She mumbles.

What's that? I ask sharply. I heard her. *Go ahead, say it again.*

I hate you.

I nod. There is no place for my rage to land, so it dies in me, temporarily causing a roar in my ears, then nothing. I feel nothing again. She's as blameless as a child. None of this will stick. We are actors, playing preposterous parts, which if I tried to write, the editor would cut, scribbling *too much,* and yes, it is, in fact, *TOO MUCH.* I also know that we aren't going to see Dr. Chan today, or any day in the future. I can't get her out of the car against her will, and I already know it's not possible to check her into detox without her consent. I can't really afford a lawyer. I want to beat traffic back up the 5 freeway and get in the bath and eat Xanax until it's dark. This is a scene that I have played before and will play again as long as I continue to want anything from her. The players' motives are clear enough: I want her to live, and she just wants to die.

Laurel Canyon, California

One time he broke into the house on Devoe Street in Brooklyn, removing the screen, scraping himself shimmying through the window. I was in the shower and screamed when he pulled back the curtain. He was ecstatic, overly proud of himself, and I laughed so hard I had to sit down. We didn't talk about us. I stayed in the shower and he watched. Didn't touch me. By dinnertime he was back in San Francisco.

In New York we met in the mornings to ride the train into the city together. He was on an extended work project and I had no fixed schedule, an interloper on the L train. I picked him up from his office at six and we'd discuss options like the train, or a ferry, or a drink. We commuted together for an entire month so we could sit side by side, hidden in plain sight. That was the month where I saw him every single day except two Sundays.

One time a plane ticket showed up in my in-box. We hadn't spoken in six weeks, not since he blocked my phone because he and his wife were on vacation. The plane ticket was audacious, a dare. *He can't be serious,* I told my friends. His smile when I arrived in Toronto with a backpack, a smile not of surprise but of confirmation: this story was about us, it would always be us.

When I was in Rome, six months into this affair, he told me he couldn't do it. He wasn't leaving her. I wept via Skype. *Why do you keep coming for me?* I asked. *Because I love you,* he said. He asked me to keep the computer on until I fell asleep and I did. He watched me, confused, and said, *I'm not sure I've ever felt as much as you do.*

Forty-eight hours later he was in Rome and I asked no questions. We kissed on a park bench in front of the Fontana Paola for over an hour, as savage as teenagers. He carried me piggyback through the streets, the gardens on top of the Gianicolo hill filling with mosquitos around us. He emptied his pockets into the Trevi Fountain and swore I would be the mother of his children.

I spent a lot of money buying us time. Whenever he failed to leave her, I booked a new ticket. I was making things easier for him, giving him space, not knowing that he's a hunter who lives for a chase.

Even now I have no doubt that everything I've suffered, every accident and pivot, from my girlhood until now, has been leading me to him.

It has crossed my mind more than once that I should not let him find me here in Laurel Canyon. And yet I'm cutting lemons on a stingingly blue morning, arranging them in a bowl, ordering singular sandwiches with extra avocado. I'm applying invisible makeup, laying out a patterned sundress because I know it will drive him insane.

We're so close to our real life. He's asked for a divorce. He's here for a job interview. He's here to see my new home, except he texts, *Our new home,* and I'm so scared that it was a typo I write, *Ha.* I tell myself that I won't remember any of the pain. That we are going through a transformation of which amnesia is a blessed side effect.

I make the man behind the counter re-wrap the sandwiches because the first job was messy. It's something the Monster's wife would know, how to order his sandwich. I had to order better than her. That's easy enough because I am uniquely adept at loving him. I am uniquely adept at dividing him into things his wife knows, and things I know. *Don't lie to me*, I told him at the beginning. *I can stomach anything but lies.*

And when he tells me that he never lies to me, though I see him lie to everyone else, I believe him.

The Monster enjoys his sandwich. He doesn't give a shit what's on it. He takes a work call and I thoughtlessly undo his pants while he talks. *Thoughtlessly*. No, I can't get away with that. I am full of thoughts. Thoughts of us referring to this blow job that he got while he was taking a meeting, when we're growing old together and the patina of this affair's misery has shifted to something bronze and noble.

When I come, I cry. When he comes, I cry again. When he tells me, with his pants still off, that he has to go pick up his wife at the airport because they're going to Palm Springs with a group of friends, *it was planned a while ago*, I don't cry.

Sooner is better, I say. *No one can live like this.*

I know, he says, looking at his hands, his ring. *I can't do this anymore.*

When? I ask.

Soon. Really soon.

Soon, someday, maybe, our refrain. *Probably this weekend*, I think. Probably when they get home from this weekend. He'll start a fight, he'll be distant. Then he'll say that he needs space. Or maybe he'll just dive in: *There's something I need to tell you.*

Let's walk, I say.

We walk up Runyon Canyon and the night cools. I think he must notice that my legs are brown. I've been running obsessively. I look around at people hiking, sweating, talking into Bluetooth headsets, tethered to their animals, and I think about their small, weak lives, and I think, *He picked me because I'm strong.*

He picked me. No, I can't get away with that either. I picked him too.

I'm late, he says.

You're having an affair, you're always late. I stall. *You don't want to come back and shower?*

No, I really have to go, he says, and checks his phone. His background photo is of her at a concert and I still don't cry. Numb, numb, numb, a breeze passes and my skirt flies up, and I will myself to be light. I'm not.

You're going to go meet your wife with my pussy all over your face?

He looks at me seriously, like I'm trespassing, but doesn't respond.

That's who you are now? I say, with more force. *You don't care enough about either of us to clean up?*

He doesn't respond, and I hear, faintly from myself, *That's who he always was.* He kisses me and I smell our sex on his lips, his cheeks, his eyelids, his earlobes.

He says something unnecessarily cruel, cruel to me, cruel to her, so shocking it's funny, and gets into his car.

I laugh. I'm charmed by how he seems unafraid of being ugly. Charmed by how messy our sex is, like we're drawing outside the lines, and all the degrading things we say and do seem to be closer to the truth of human nature. Charmed, perhaps by our superiority, though it feels to me as the months go on that I've made a terrible mistake. I can't dwell on it, only continue soldiering on. I let him go and I drive up to Mulholland. I continue dividing my life into Times I Cried, Times I Didn't Cry. I drive with the heater on and the windows down until the San Fernando Valley turns blue, then black, and the lights come on.

Death Valley, California

It's us and about one million other tourists descending on Death Valley for the rare burst of fertility and color called a "superbloom." I've never had the desire to go to Death Valley (*Something about the name,* I tell the Love Interest on the drive), and, to be honest, I don't have the desire to go camping (*I have my period,* I tell him. *You can't camp when you have your period?* he asks. *Not really?*). The Love Interest is a passionate outdoorsman, and I have purported to be one as well. I'm fucked.

The entire park is full (*Even the hotels?* I ask musically, and he thinks I'm joking), so we head out to BLM land outside the park bounds. This place is not Joshua Tree. It's blanched, as if ill, and featureless. As soon as we find a spot—the spot is not exactly beautiful but is technically outdoors, so it's still part of "the experience"—it starts to rain. The temperature drops and the rain turns to needles.

Is this snow? I ask. I'm shivering. I had to borrow his socks, I'm so unprepared.

The Love Interest shrugs, *Maybe hail?* And keeps setting up our tent.

I'm wondering how embarrassed I'll be when I ask to sleep in the car. His girlfriend—or whatever she is—definitely loves to camp. She loves to rock climb and probably howls at the moon with abandon, has passages of *Women Who Run with the Wolves* memorized.

I have a hard time explaining to the Love Interest how tired I get. He says, *From what?* As if exhaustion has an addressable root cause or could be remedied by sleep. *Depression,* I told him, just one time, to see how it landed. He kind of laughed. I watch him bring firewood out of the trunk into the rain.

You can't build a fire in this, I say, waving my hand to the weather. I notice a sour taste in my mouth that means I'm very, very close to ruining this "experience."

I can, he says. For the next fifteen minutes I bite my tongue so hard it bleeds, sitting silently, waiting for him to give up as the rain extinguishes every effort. Then there is a roaring, orange-tongued fire.

I'm impressed.

Though I initially called bullshit on his open relationships, it's true. His girlfriend, or his primary, knows that he's seeing me. She knows who I am, that he and I have friends in common. Knows that he's camping with me right now. He's not sure exactly how polyamory works, *very much a work in progress,* but believes in the honesty and communication it requires. He believes in questioning all his assumptions. Up until now, I've either not cared or pretended not to care. I have told him that I'm *in something* also, but I don't talk about it. Now I'm here with him, outside my comfort zone, and it strikes me that this is how you build things. After this weekend, the Love Interest and I will have stories, tellable stories, ones not about hotel rooms and how one sneaks in and out of crowded places. The night sky crackles as the clouds

recede, my hands burn from the fire. I drink red wine, he drinks
mescal and I am so fucking relieved to be out of the city.

I don't like open things, I say, suddenly.

What?

Open relationships. They're dumb. Don't work. Sometimes when I
talk about my feelings out loud, my vocabulary regresses to that
of a seven-year-old.

You've had experience with them?

I've had experience cheating.

So you already know that monogamy is flawed.

Ha. I take another drink. *Yes, it's flawed.*

*And you think those two things, open relationships and cheating,
are the same thing?*

I know this debate inside and out, and I'm usually partial to
late-night philosophical chats about monogamy. I've studied infi-
delity, polyamory, and I did try an open relationship in college
after I read too much Sartre (it didn't end well). I've questioned
heteronormative assumptions and forced myself into threesomes,
foursomes. Part of me wants to unleash a deluge of cynicism on
him, make him feel embarrassed by whatever he's trying with
his girlfriend. But the truth is, I don't know what I want. I'm still
waiting for the Monster.

It just doesn't feel good. Knowing you're with someone else.

Why?

Because I don't like it.

What don't you like about it?

It's not fucking cute, I say. I'm mad, grossly mad, indicating a
well of feeling. *I'm not one of those flexible girls, open to whatever-
the-fuck experience. I'm a fucking adult. You can't commit to this
girl*—what is she, twenty-two? *So open-minded?*—so you're keeping

your options open under the guise of enlightenment, but as soon as either one of you falls in love, the entire enterprise falls apart.

He exhales. *Maybe. What are you saying?*

I don't know.

It's been dark almost the entire time we've been here. I haven't seen any flowers. There was a poster when we were denied entrance to the park, drawn in a 1950s tourism style that said, *Death Valley: Remember, at the lowest point in North America, the sky begins at your feet!* It depicts two people standing at the valley floor and the stars rippling up from the ground. It's like that now, stars all the way to my frozen toes.

Have you ever been in love? I ask him.

I think so.

Then you haven't. It's hard enough with just two people.

Are you asking me to stop seeing her?

That would be crazy. I can't promise this man anything. I'm not even sure how I feel about him. And the hideous thought comes to me that perhaps I don't like this arrangement because it's too . . . *honest.* This rage coming off me is so mis-projected, so directly related to this affair I'm trapped in, that I can hear the Monster laughing at me. And yet, I feel a surety I'm not used to, which is, *I'm not doing this again.* Nothing murky or illegible. Nothing where we parcel out our hearts and give only to withdraw. *I won't.*

What are you saying? he asks again because I've gone quiet.

I don't like it. That's all. I think in order for things to have a shot, you have to take risks. Monogamy is a great big risk.

His face has grown serious in the firelight. This is it, the night he figures out that I'm not worth the effort. Fuck. He has no idea what to say.

Anaheim, California

The Love Interest doesn't scare easily. Weeks later, walking his dog at a park near his house, he asks me, *Was it always bad with your mom?*

He knows that I've been parentless for a long time, that my stories have calcified. He knows I'm writing a piece about my father and the writing causes me a lot of pain. I'm surprised by his question, by his relentless pursuit of some positive. At that moment, I can't remember her, really remember her as a mother. Her disabilities color every memory.

Not always bad, but always hard, I say.

His question causes me to recall suddenly and perfectly a day she picked us up from day care late. We were the last kids. My sullenness on the car ride home. I know it was winter because it felt like it had been dark for hours, adding insult to injury. I didn't look up for a long time. When I did, I noticed we were not heading toward home. In the front seat my mother drove silently, chauffeuring us as she did every day of her life.

Where are we going? I whined.

Dinner, she said.

We never went out to eat. We didn't have that kind of money.

It was seven p.m., the time when she normally microwaved us fish sticks, or, if she was particularly spent, turned the car into the drive-through line at McDonald's. It was almost time for our one hour of television.

Somewhere on the 5 freeway she handed back two annual passes to Disneyland. They were a gift from my aunt. I think it so kind now, that my aunt had my mother give them to us. We screamed.

We walked into the park, lights twinkling, walked down the vanilla-scented facsimile of America's Main Street, veering left through Adventureland. We sprinted, knowing the layout by heart, the park crowds thinned out because of the lateness of the hour.

We had a dinner reservation at the Blue Bayou, the restaurant inside Pirates of the Caribbean. It was a restaurant where it was always a humid buzzing night, fireflies and cicadas. Water knocked against the boats, a robot man rocked pensively on his porch, beyond that more silhouettes of placidity. I ordered a French Dip sandwich and French fries.

I haven't thought about this in years, I tell the Love Interest. I think of my mother sitting at her desk in the courtroom and calling. A private smile on her lips as she drove through the dark to get us. I think of the way the little anxieties of her day were nonexistent to us. I remember telling my elementary school friends about this dinner at the Blue Bayou as proof against our household's brokenness.

I held on to my mother's hand as we exited, far past our bedtime, and I cried. Already conscious of how time wrapped around loss, I wailed. It was over and already fading. I would never get back that surprise and gratitude. When I cried as a child, I was sure it would go on forever, that no one and nothing could stop it, or I might not come back. I held tight to my mother and cried, *That was the best day of my life.*

How's your mom? Carly asks. I consider telling her the truth.

She's fine, I say. *The same.*

That is part of the truth. My mother is always the same. There's part of the story that's missing, part that I can almost get away with not telling. But then everything would continue as a half-truth, a not-so-accidental omission. And I will be just like my parents.

Though they'd been together for years and had a child, Carly didn't marry Alejandro until 2013, in a wedding under a spread of redwoods in the Carmel Valley. I flew in from New York, my brand-new divorce belied by my long hair cut into a severe bob. Before I drove up to Carmel, I decided to stay with my aunt for a night. And I asked her if she would drive me to meet my mom for a pedicure.

My mother did get better in those intervening years. She walked without a cane or walker. She dragged her foot a bit, but she continued acupuncture. Her hair grew in and she could visit a salon to keep it blond. Around 2010, she was able to work part-time at Home Depot at the register—it only lasted about two months, but still. For a moment she was conversant with the world, could ask a coworker how the weekend was. She volunteered to hold babies at the hospital. She attended AA meetings, where she met Larry. She went to church every Sunday with my grandfather. After Home Depot didn't work out, she stopped most of that. She pulled inward. She drank, then had her first spell in rehab post-aneurysm. But she still drove.

During those strong years, my grandfather found a doctor who would sign off on giving her a license. My mother's car was outfitted with the gas pedal on the left side because her right side was still extremely weak after being paralyzed. I suppose it was justified. She didn't drive on the freeways. If she could run a cash register, she had the mental wherewithal comparable to the senior citizens who lived around Seal Beach and still lumbered their behemoth sedans around town.

The day before Carly's wedding, my aunt dropped me off at the nail salon on Main Street in Seal Beach. My mother drove herself to meet me. Though she had had her license for quite a few years, I had never been in a car with her. I refused. I openly criticized my aunt and grandfather for enabling her driving. But that day I conceded to have my mother drop me off at my aunt's after the pedicure, so my aunt didn't have to wait around for us.

My mother and I sat in cracked old massage chairs getting pedicures and my mother held my hand. She was chirpy. She told the pedicurist that I was married, and I didn't correct her. *I'm waiting for grandbabies*, she whispered, and giggled, covering her mouth.

She had a really difficult time with the shoe on her right foot when we were trying to leave the salon. I saw a flutter of panic in her. Was it me? Just my presence? She had parked at a forty-five-degree angle in one of the spots lining Main Street. It required her to reverse out of the spot and then pull forward into the street. She was shaking when we got in the car with lacquered toes. She didn't seem to know how to use the push-button ignition. I offered to get out of the car and guide her back into the street, to pause oncoming traffic for her.

I stood in the street. There were no cars coming. I waved for her to back up. Her car shot into reverse, barely missing me. I remember thinking, *Something's gone wrong.* The car flew faster, backward, picking up speed, down the street, before I saw my mother's panicked face and watched her spin the wheel. The car careened sharply—backward—up the sidewalk, then through the plate glass of a floral shop window. The glass exploded and then came the crunch of metal as the car finally stopped. A second of quiet and blooms falling.

No, I said out loud. Then again, *No, no, no, no, no,* as I ran. Pedestrians and people from inside other stores and coffee shops were shouting, rushing in from the street. *Here it is,* I thought. *She's dead.*

She wasn't. She was probably going only twenty-five or thirty miles an hour. But as I ran up, a man was clutching his forearm, bleeding on the sidewalk in front of the floral store. He had been walking on the street, my mother's car flying in front of him, but the glass had hit him. A surface wound. There were two women on the floor of the shop, holding each other and crying. Above them was the car. The way she backed into the place, the trunk of the car was almost vertical against the wall, the front of the car pointed down to the ground. And there was my mother, intact, flapping her hands in front of her horrified face.

I climbed up on a table and undid the driver's side door. I unbuckled her seat belt and pulled her down. Her legs gave out immediately, and I dragged her to the corner. I ran my hands over her face, her neck, her stomach for wounds, checking for blood.

Oh no, she said softly. She repeated it. Her eyes couldn't land on anything.

You're alive, I said. I held on to her hands and burst into tears.

She looked at me and saw me, recognized that I was her daughter. She said, *Do you think they're going to take my license?*

Shut up, I said. I shook her violently. *Shut up. I'm calling your sister.*

My mom bit on her cuticles, scared. *Just don't call Daddy.*

The woman who owned the store was hysterical. The car had gone above her—she had crouched down behind the register desk, which my mother drove over. It had forced the car upward as opposed to crushing this woman against the wall. The street was chaos. Ambulances arrived quickly, followed by the local news. The floral shop was new in Seal Beach, owned by a married couple. The husband had been getting coffee with his two children a few doors down. They had all been in the store one minute earlier. He ran in, eyes wide at the damage, then put his arms around his wife, pulling her off the ground to him. He found us, stood over my mother, and screamed. I don't remember what he said, but I remember I was curled around her, hiding her from him, and his spit was falling on me, or maybe it was his tears.

She's handicapped, I screamed at him, keeping my head down. The only thing I remember him saying was that he was going to lock her up. I screamed: *I'm going to put you in fucking jail if you don't back the fuck up.* He threw a gingham towel at the wall next to my head and walked away. His wife, the one who had narrowly missed a critical injury, came over and apologized. She held my mother's hand and asked to pray with her. She rocked back and forth on her heels as she did.

Then my aunt arrived with my grandfather. My mother was sitting in a corner of the store with a cup of water given to her by the paramedics. I went to my aunt, this woman who used to survey homicide victim photos with her coffee. She was the most shaken I've ever seen her. She held her hand over her mouth. My grandfather maybe blinked twice. He didn't speak the entire time he was there.

Did she hurt anyone? my aunt said quietly from behind her hand.

No, I said. *Just a scratch on that guy over there.* The paramedics had already wrapped him up. *But there were kids. In here. Just a minute before.*

I couldn't look at the children. They were six and nine. They clung to their mother. They were captivated by the broken glass, by the wrecked furniture and flowers, by the vertical car. I had stopped crying at that point, but when I saw them, my stomach crowded into my throat.

Then we're saved, my aunt said. All practicality. She talked to the cops, then the owners, exchanged phone numbers, and she loaded my mother into an ambulance. Even as my mother was strapped in and given oxygen, she had no idea what happened. She couldn't explain why she didn't use the brakes or couldn't remember how her car worked. She didn't know enough to apologize.

My aunt drove me to her house, and we didn't talk for the short drive. When we walked in, my uncle poured me a gigantic glass of white wine though it wasn't noon yet. I held perfectly still.

I'm sorry, my aunt said. My uncle was speechless.

No more, I thought. I can't be accountable for my mother's negligence, or for the benign neglect that we call *care* in this family. I skittered around my guilt, the thought of those children. I wanted to scream, *I knew she shouldn't be driving,* but I would get no relief from being correct. *Where are the adults,* I wondered? I felt panic sitting in my aunt's house as if I were lingering too long at the scene of a crime.

I'm going. I finished the wine. *To the wedding.*

I ran. I would not visit my mother in the hospital that afternoon. I would not stay in Long Beach another second. I took my

grandfather's car, which I didn't know would be my car someday, and I drove six hours to Carmel. I collapsed on Carly's hotel
doorstep at ten p.m. and she put me in a robe and asked over and
over, *Are you okay?*

I don't think so, I said. *But I got out of there.*

Never mind that the small turn toward self-preservation was
met by acts of self-destruction. I got so drunk at the wedding I
vomited all over a Balenciaga dress that Carly's sister loaned me. I
continued to be so drunkenly sick that Alex had to skip the after-
party and take care of me. I slept on the floor of the bathroom in
Alex's hotel room and promised to pay her back but knew I could
never. All my ex-boyfriends were there and I flirted with them
brutally, ignoring their new girlfriends or wives. Never mind that
Brad had RSVP'd for the wedding with me but was no longer
my husband, or that I was a waitress and a grad student with a
part of a novel written and a shit ton of debt. One week prior I
would have said that this optimistic leap into a new life was cause
for celebration. Now I couldn't remember why I had taken this
senseless risk; it was a low I would never recover from. The bile
stuck to my teeth tasted like failure. Never mind that all I could
think on the drive to and from Carmel was that someday I was
going to die and that day couldn't come soon enough.

I'm still on the phone with Carly, staring up at a line of grim
eucalyptuses. I'm in Laurel Canyon. It's 2015. I say, *It's unbearable, actually. My mother. The pain I feel thinking about her, let
alone seeing her, is intolerable and I would do anything not to feel it.*

I wonder why you chose them, Carly says. *Nancy and Stephen.*

I didn't, I say. I didn't ask to be born to them.

*We all chose our parents. They're the first lesson we have to learn.
They're our teachers.*

You're getting so weird, I say. But how deeply have I armored myself that something so obvious is shocking to me?

Here is one thing I know about writing: it sometimes happens that previously unconnected items seem to me connected (instinctively, definitively). I wonder how they got entwined that way. I try to identify these filaments between moments, which I believe will lead me to a conclusion, something satisfying for all. Every time I fail to answer whatever call first woke me in the night, and whatever my body knows remains mute to my mind, I am left with the moments, strung together with elliptical logic if any. The blind leading the blind, is how I feel when I am nursing my mother and when I am trying to untangle the mess love has made of me.

God, how I envy my mother's lack of memory.

PART II

Father

Long Beach, California

In the winter of 1983, my mother gave birth to me, clasped me to her chest, went blind with love, and called me Jessie. It was short for Jessica, the name she had chosen for me. She had told the family, *If I have a girl, she's going to be Jessie.* There is—in the boxes in my garage—an engraved silver rattle that says *Jessica*.

Outside the hospital room my father—who was at dinner when I came screaming into the world, fighting my swaddle from the first second—filled out forms, including my birth certificate. He named me Stephanie. After himself, Stephen. He had, after all, been hoping I would be a boy. Was he sober that night? Or was he, for one moment, just a father, bowled over by the phenomenon of childbirth? He let my mom call me Jessica for a full day before he told her she was wrong.

Washington

Right around the time I was moving back to California, my paternal uncle died under puzzling circumstances.

It appeared he drove his motorcycle into a ravine in Washington State. Then that explanation seemed too simple and too brutal. There was a rumor that he was playing chicken with some men in a pickup truck. But what is a man in his late sixties doing playing chicken? There are skid marks, but what do they really indicate beyond hesitation? The official report called it an accident. The obituary said, *Bill was certainly happy that morning when he took his motorcycle to the open road . . .*

Bill was my father's older brother. They had a falling-out when I was sixteen and living with my father in Colorado. I rarely saw my uncle, though he lived near us. My father—in those years—had a lot of falling-outs with people. Supervisors, his longtime girlfriend, doctors, his sister who lived with us for a time. My aunt filled up her car and left, literally, in the middle of the night. I saw those breaks as a warning, a reminder to the daughter he left behind, that he could walk away from anyone and anything.

There is a grave in San Pedro, California, marked with the name of my father's younger brother, Phillip. He was one of six healthy, bronzed children born to Gloria and my grandfather Bill. By the time I was born, Phillip was gone and five siblings remained.

I learned about grief that works like a cancer by staring at a photo of Phillip's tombstone, surrounded by the hands of his parents and siblings, kept in my paternal grandfather's house. *Who*, I wondered as a child, *kept a framed photo of a tombstone?* The photo was a laceration that could never be spoken of directly.

When I asked my mother and aunt about him, they—who never hesitated to denigrate my father—just sucked in their lips and shook their heads. *It broke them*, my mother said, which was as close as she came to compassion for her ex-in-laws. I don't know exactly what happened (Haven't I asked before? When did I give up on figuring out the truth?), but I do know that Phillip was on the back of a motorcycle driven by his eldest brother, Bill.

I know my father, Stephen, was in a car with my grandfather. Had they been racing, the car and the motorcycle? A whisper that Bill, driving the motorcycle, had been drinking. I heard once that there was an item (a hat? sunglasses?) dropped and Bill turned the bike around to retrieve it. I heard my father saw the entire thing from the car with his father. That he could never un-see it.

I know Phillip was sixteen years old when he flew off the back of Bill's motorcycle and hit the freeway, dead.

Bill was certainly happy that morning . . . Now when I ask my aunts and cousins what really happened, with either Phillip or Bill, I get a slightly different, sometimes a wildly different, story. This makes sense. No one wants to look directly at the trauma itself, only the shapes it makes.

My sister is under the impression that we should try to go west for Bill's funeral (not that we necessarily do it, but that we appear to be trying seems important). I am busy. I'm packing up my life in New York, I'm moving to Los Angeles, I have a wedding in Mexico, did she not remember that?

Besides, *I haven't seen our father in six years, do you think it's an accident?* I ask her. It's a rhetorical question. Historically, she's been more forgiving of him. I think it's because she doesn't know him as well.

The last time I saw my father was a courtesy to her: it was her wedding. To imagine sitting next to him at his brother's funeral, having to witness the Catholic theatrics, being close to his pain again, a pain that is, in fact, endless, all the while pretending to be his daughter, is physically impossible for me. I skip the funeral, go to Mexico instead. But the spell is broken. I can feel him again. It's in Mexico that I start writing about him.

San Pedro, California

The men came from San Pedro.

My father, my ghost uncles, my aunt's husband, Gary, my former stepfather, Richard. On the other side of the Palos Verdes Peninsula is the Port of Los Angeles, so industrial it looks postapocalyptic in places. There's a point, driving on the Vincent Thomas Bridge, where the burned bark smell of the refineries used to creep into the car. Christina and I would scream and plug our noses. Rising above the bay where every freighter, cruise ship, ocean-bound import and export exchanged their identities, is a hill called San Pedro.

As in most transitional areas, immigrant communities thrived in port cities, the strongest of them being the Italians and Croatians (from both of whom I can claim descent, depending on whom you ask). San Pedro remains one of the most ethnically diverse cities in the county of Los Angeles. The Catholic working class still organize their bands of formally dressed children to church on Sundays. The city is a gritty twin to Palos Verdes with its Protestant, country-club citizens. And in my father's day, as a Palos Verdes girl's life marched toward her debutante ball, her eventual marriage and procreation, a Pedro boy's life marched toward the holiest of all grails, joining the longshoremen's union.

Not my father's though. His marched toward Oxford, an MBA, a major job at Ball Aerospace, owning multiple homes, juggling multiple lives. He was too golden.

He left us when I was three years old. Or my mother kicked him out. Or he went to rehab. Or my grandfather kicked him out. Or, as he would say to me years later: *To be honest, I never had much interest in children.*

My father has never been around one of his three children for an extended period of time. He rarely remembered to call for a birthday or purchase a Christmas present. I was ten when we finally started to visit him regularly, at his new home in Boulder, Colorado. My mother was surprised when he offered to take us for eight weeks of summer. My sister and I flew on an airplane by ourselves, the flight attendants hovering over us. My father set himself up in a small town outside of Boulder called Lyons, abutting the Rockies, with a beautiful wife and a sparkling, cream-cheeked baby boy, my half brother, Jared. But on those summer visits, he put us directly into an outdoor adventure camp. He said he was curing us of the corruption of the country club my maternal grandparents belonged to, but it meant that we hardly saw him during those two months.

When I became his child full-time at age sixteen, he had been away for the majority of my life. We knew nothing about each other. He put me into a devastatingly expensive school where he hoped they would do the heavy lifting of containing me. He had no interest in starting a career in parenting with me, which was fine as I didn't have any interest in being parented.

What I knew about his cocaine use from my aunt was dismissed—in my mind—as recreational. Youthful indiscretion.

Even before the full extent of his addiction came to light when I was a senior in college, he wasn't like a father. But it was during my two years in Boulder, against odds or sense, that I came to adore him.

He had that gilded, incorrigible quality that women went crazy for. His charm was legendary. He could talk to anyone. He gave impromptu speeches that were rhyming poems and moved his audiences to tears. He hunted, he fished, he hiked. He was grand and masculine. He was smart and condescending—dismissive in a way that never seemed closed-minded, just final. Accordingly, the women in his life stopped fighting quickly.

I began to take pride in being able to tolerate what many women eventually found intolerable. I didn't ask questions. I never pursued him. I never tried to connect. I would laugh when he hurt me. I wasn't his kid, I was the person that understood him. I was the only one who understood that he couldn't love anyone, especially not me, and I was charmed by his cruelty. The endless game of earning his affection. I began to think of myself as tough. It doesn't seem like a crime—but it's easy to see I was built to love a certain kind of man.

Owens Valley, California

The Love Interest and I are driving along the San Bernardino freeway where it splits the desert. We are heading to Joshua Tree again. It turns out, I love camping.

He's picked me up from Alex's bachelorette in Palm Springs. I have glitter in my hair and four false eyelashes left. I'm so hungover I'm nearly fetal. When I climb into the front seat, there's a bottle of water and a cup with wildflowers in it. He calls it *a car bouquet*. I feel girlish and grateful. I've pitched an essay, unformulated still, about this California he's given me access to. I want his help but don't know how to ask for it.

I want to say that the desiccation of Owens Lake is the greatest environmental disaster in California's history, I tell him.

The greatest? he asks, skeptical. *Is that true?*

I don't know. It feels true.

Maybe you should do some research before you write something like that. I can put you in touch with one of my professors.

No. I'm annoyed. *Never mind.*

I put my hand on the window. Heat ripples against the glass, the wind turbines moving plaintively through it.

He says, *You want general permission to write whatever feels true?*

A few weeks ago, on the tail end of our Death Valley trip, the Love Interest took me to see a piece of land art at Owens Lake. I'd never heard of the place, but he once worked on a ranch overlooking it. This part of California's Central Valley, laid between the Mojave Desert and the Sierra Nevadas, is a tourist stop for those on their way to Mount Whitney. The area is more famous for its economic depression and for making good meth. As we came into the valley and found the Sierras extending sharply into the horizon, I saw what looked like a massive scab on the valley floor.

I scanned the landscape. *Where's the lake?*

There's no lake. That's the point.

At the end of the nineteenth century, Owens Lake was one of the largest in the state, the surrounding area so lush it was once referred to as the Switzerland of California. Known for its whitecaps from the Sierra winds, the lake floated two steamships that transported silver from the mines between the Sierras and Inyo Mountains. By 1926, hardly more than a decade after the Los Angeles Aqueduct was completed, taking water south to feed the thriving metropolis, Owens Lake was completely dry.

A dry lakebed is ugly, but not a disaster. Dust is a disaster. Carcinogenic, powder-fine, lodge-in-your-lungs-forever dust. The winds that once whipped whitecaps now blew the dust off the lakebed and scattered it across the state. In 1987, the Environmental Protection Agency called Owens Lake the worst source of dust pollution in the country. Without the Owens Valley water, the city of Los Angeles could not exist.

We drove down onto the lakebed and walked around the sculptures in Perry Cardoza's park, a large shaded plaza where visitors could take in the remains of the "lake," surrounded by "trails" that mimic the dust migration. Beyond the one shaded area, the wind and sun made it hard to linger. We were the only people around for miles. The salt-cracked lakebed spread around us, the sky unbearably bright, gravel paths marking the way to sprinklers spitting out water.

Afterward we stopped in Lone Pine for coffee. There was a road sign that said: INDEPENDENCE, CALIFORNIA, 16 MILES. *Independence.* I had seen it before and was stunned. In an unnameable part of my body, a bruise was pressed upon.

What's up? he said. This man always asked a question when I turned rigid.

I looked at the sign again. *I've been here before. A place up by Independence. I went when I was a girl.*

He waited for me to go on. I surprised myself and told the Love Interest a story:

Attached to my father's surname is an old mining claim up in the Inyo Mountains. His family has had a bare-bones cabin up there since the 1890s. The landscape of that part of the Inyos is harsh. *Rugged,* someone kinder might say.

My father's last name is a name I declined to retrieve when my marriage ended, but it remains attached to me like my Catholic schooling, my maternal grandmother's WASPiness, and being born in Los Angeles. Things I enjoy forgetting but from which I seem unable to remove myself.

In that moment, when I saw the sign for Independence, I realized I hadn't thought of the "Diggins"—as they called the camp and the land around it—in years. My sister and I visited a handful of times as children, these visits dominated by the fear we felt whenever we went anywhere with our father. He did not know how to take care of us, how to make food for us or bathe us; he didn't have games or toys.

His father's house in San Pedro, where he took us for his visits, was always dark—an Italian peasant thing, to keep the lights off and heavy curtains drawn. The men in his family hunted, and the house was filled with taxidermy: an elk head, a boar, and multiple bear rugs that shed.

Our great-grandfather, who had dementia, lived there too, and spent all of his days on a faded blue couch, staring out the window, unspeaking. It seems quaintly gothic now, but it was terrifying then. My father smelled like a man: one part aftershave, one part feral, one part rental car.

Our mother was back to being a "Ferrero." Ferrero family retreats involved Palm Desert, books, and tubes of orange-scented Bain de Soleil. When my father called to announce he was taking us to the Diggins, she shuddered. *What a godforsaken place,* she'd say. I was unsure if she meant the cabin or her marriage.

I remember the rattlesnakes. The bats at dusk. The frogs and the gigs for killing them, the rats' nests we discovered, the guns we used for target practice, and the truckloads of illegal fireworks our father shot off, their explosions thrilling us. We all slept outside, my sister and I horrified as the coyotes' yips and howls clocked the night.

The adults kept a variety of rusty Jeeps and Land Cruisers on the property. My father would let me sit on his lap and steer over the roadless brush. He collected the rattles off dead snakes in the road and kept them in the cup holder, where they jumped each time he accelerated.

There were cousins, nine of us in total, along with diaphanous aunts who made a warm band into which my sister and I wanted to be absorbed. After a day or two, we didn't want to leave the

Diggins. It also held a treacherous promise: that I would—if I was strong enough, shot straight enough, did not complain while hiking—be accepted back into my father's life. Even as a six-year-old, I was addicted to this challenge. Every time he left, I had failed.

Colorado

There is a rehab center tucked into the mountains outside of Estes Park, Colorado, a town known as the gateway to the Rockies. It must be eight years ago now that Christina and I flew in from New York City and drove through a snowstorm to spend a "healing" weekend with my father, who was finishing up his thirty days.

For years my paternal grandmother, Gloria, had been saying that my father was not a drug addict but suffered from bipolar disorder. The last hospital he was admitted to was inclined to agree. They put him on Lithium and Thorazine, but the two drugs weren't mixing well. He had better diction after a bottle of gin than he did with the pills.

While the patients went through their own closing ceremony, the families sat on plastic chairs in a semicircle around a space heater with the other family members. They were haggard parents, bereft siblings, thickened men and women aged before their time by dealing with their addicts.

We went around the circle and told our stories. My sister and I were at the end. We listened to the thefts, the car crashes, the lies, the injuries, the unimaginable actualized over and over again. I started thinking about which story about my father I would tell these exhausted people. I thought I would do the hard talking for my sister.

I come from a long line of charismatic liars, I might say. *Our main currencies are epiphanies and promises, highly inflated, though we ourselves remain completely bankrupt . . .*

Some writerly grandiose bullshit like that. My turn came and I remember getting out, *My father is a liar* before I erupted into tears.

That was only his fifth relapse.

When it comes to my father, I don't believe addiction is a disease. I don't necessarily believe he's bipolar. I don't believe he can be treated for any of the afflictions that we hope will explain his atrocious behavior. In my time with addicts I've learned to identify those that are liars first, those whose great comfort in addiction is that it allows them to practice their art. It was clear, as I watched him sleepwalk through his graduation from rehab, that it was not drugs that brought him here. It's what I call his black hole. It sits behind his heart. It has been threatening him his entire life. Drugs are just one way to pacify it.

I know because I'm his daughter. He passed it on to me. I realize during these visits that I have been guarding against it, minute by minute, for my entire life. I've touched all its edges.

———

An attaché case left on the roof of a silver car, flying past the gray strip malls of Southern California. It belongs to my father, coming to pick us up and take us out to dinner. Perpetually tanned in tailored Italian suits, a different rental car every visit. He was always on his way to and from the airport, never in my life for more than forty-eight hours at a time. I couldn't keep track of where he lived, but I believe, after he left us, he went to New Mexico, then Seattle, Washington, eventually Colorado. He told me he made telescopes for outer space. I told my friends, their parents, my teachers: my father is just away on a business trip. The teachers told my mother, and she said, *What your father tells you isn't true.*

Fifteen years or so later when I was not a child, my father and I were at a gas station a few hours outside of St. Louis. I was on my way to my senior year at college. My father's cell phone died and he made us pull over so he could use the pay phone. I had no idea who he was calling. He asked me for change. I fidgeted in the gummy leather seat, annoyed that we could only agree on Bob Dylan to listen to. My father's attaché case was on the front seat. I wonder now: If I had opened it back then, would I have found him out? Would I have done anything differently?

Instead I looked at the attaché case and remembered the time he left it on the roof of the car when I was a child. When he pulled up to my mother's house in Long Beach, my sister and I were out front waiting for him. My mother wouldn't let him come past the front gate. He opened the car door with a huge smile for us and then he saw the attaché on the roof. I remember thinking that he was more excited to see it than us, that his relief was audible, so marked a thermometer could have picked up the change in him.

His attaché case was the eloquent extension of his arm. He said, *Let me see, where is my attaché,* to any question asked of him. He would undo the clasps and consult a calendar while we sat at Chuck E. Cheese and I told him how good I was at tetherball. His importance was bigger than games and rides at Chuck E. Cheese. It was bigger than my mother, my sister, and me combined.

On that drive back to Ohio, I knew my father was unwell.

I think I knew, subconsciously, that I shouldn't be in the car with him. I did not imagine that his life as he had meticulously constructed it was coming to an end. That his mysteries that enthralled me were the most mundane lies.

What I'm left with from that drive is this image of him at the pay phone: He is so tall that he can't fit in the phone booth. He is so thin he looks like a plank of lumber. He is looking at his hands as he speaks; he is still so tan he looks golden against the blue Midwest flatland behind him that goes on and on and on.

When I tell people I lived in Boulder, Colorado, I don't actually mean Boulder. I mean Hygiene, a petite unincorporated town outside of Boulder, where the foothills flatten, where my father had a home. Hygiene got its name from the tuberculosis sanatorium built there in 1881 (called the "Hygiene House," which is also what we called my father's house), during a time when it is estimated that one-third of Colorado's residents were there because of some illness to be cleansed by the thin mountain air.

Hygiene is a stop sign on a country road, surrounded by lakes, rivers, small ranches, and rutted roads that take you toward the Rockies. It is a small market, an elementary school, a post office, and a gas station. The gas station was important to me because I could walk there and rent from their small collection of VHS tapes. My father didn't believe in "having a television," but we did have a small television with no channels (no cable or Internet when I moved in) and a dusty VCR that lay next to it. He wouldn't even keep it in the house. It was kept on the screened porch, even in winter.

The man who ran the gas station was what is generously

referred to as a "local character" or what I, at sixteen, referred to as a "hick." He had a glass eye, bad teeth, and a prominent mustache. He and my father were friends because the gas station had a secret collection of illegal cigars. While I browsed the same thirty VHS tapes, wondering what I could possibly watch, yet again, he would take my father into the back room for "the Cubans." Occasionally they would smoke one together, and I would stand outside talking with people filling up their tanks or walk over to the cemetery next door where the graves were so old the names were rubbed out. I imagined that many of them met their end at the Hygiene House, which promised a curative elixir of mineral water that was actually just water pumped from a ditch out back.

Later Mr. Glass Eye hired Blake, a teenager my age who would end up robbing the store and running away before he could graduate from high school, a beautiful boy who claimed to be the only mixed-race kid in Colorado. One day I left school early so I could get home in time to work a closing shift at the coffee shop in Boulder. I took my dad's truck to the gas station to fill up, and Blake and I chatted. He asked some questions about the private school I went to, what the kids were like. *The usual: boring, spoiled,* was my response. He said he was finishing his shift and asked if I wanted to get high. With an eight-hour shift ahead of me, one that got me home past midnight, I of course did.

We drove in his truck to what I assumed to be his home, but as we went through the side gate, I saw it was an empty model home: generic marble in the kitchen, dustless fixtures. This was something I did a lot back in Seal Beach—we broke into empty houses, threw parties where we knew a family would be out of town, hopped fences for swimming pools. In California my old friends were thinning out—some were pregnant, some were in juvenile detention centers, two boys in my grade had died. I remember feeling comforted to be back with a "public school" kid when I was with Blake. Not for the criminal element exactly, but because here was someone whose life had limits like my own. He had to work through high school. Someone who didn't just talk about whether to hit their vacation home in Breck or Vail when the powder came.

The other thing about Blake: he was smart. He was the only person I knew in Colorado who had also read Nietzsche. And he didn't like Kerouac, which made us both pariahs in high school. We chatted about college, which we both believed to be a scam, although he had these "crazy test scores" that meant he could go "just about" anywhere he wanted. I had pretty surprising test scores myself, considering I had taken Vicodin a half hour before my SATs. As we talked, he rolled a joint and put a line of white powder on top of it. I didn't ask, I still don't know.

Fifteen minutes later I was on the floor, paralyzed. Blake was talking me through it, but he was above water, and I was under it. I remember flashes of fear feeling like faraway lightning, muted. The fear wasn't about being sexually threatened by Blake. I think now—though I couldn't have articulated it at the time—that I knew Blake was gay. The fear—if I could have accessed it—was that I had taken a lot of drugs at that point, and this was one I couldn't stay ahead of. He took me back to my dad's truck and drove me home. He graciously pulled over and patted my back while I puked. He got me up the stairs to my bedroom, where I remembered, belatedly, that I had work. *You have to call*, I said thickly. *I'm lost*. I remember saying that over and over again. The world was strange, a map I couldn't read anymore. It was at that moment, when he had deposited me safely on the carpet in my bedroom and handed me the cordless phone, that he bolted.

I didn't call work. I called my father at work. Repeatedly, because he didn't pick up the first time. *I'm sick,* I said. *I have to go to the hospital.* He told me that he was in the middle of a busy day, that if what I said was true to call an ambulance. He was impatient. I got embarrassed and told him I was fine. I don't know how time passed, or whether it did, but I was in the same spot on the carpet, holding the phone, when he got home after dark.

It turns out the man who owned the gas station, Mr. Glass Eye, hired Blake for a reason. He was good at drugs. They ran them out of the back room where they kept the Cubans. Weed, pills, cocaine. And it turns out that Mr. Glass Eye, and even Blake eventually, had been supplying my father with ever-increasing amounts of crystal meth for years.

———

Living with my father in Colorado meant no curfew. No real supervision. It meant a tongue piercing at sixteen, all I had to do was make out with the piercer for a minute. It meant a pedophilic old man at the liquor store who would let me buy booze if I let him listen to me pee. It meant driving my aunt's Volvo wasted, a friend puking out the window, streaking the car, thus christening it "Old Pukey" forevermore. It meant that my private school friends didn't know about ecstasy, but I taught them very quickly. It meant raves in the mountains, in the fields, in warehouses in Denver. It meant a thirty-five-hour-a-week job at a café, one that left me red-eyed for school the next day. It meant going through bottles of NyQuil every week, before transitioning to Ambien.

Private school was like day care: I talked back to the dean, the headmaster, took long lunches and went to tanning beds. I laughed off math class though it meant—as a senior—I was taking class with freshmen. It meant mountain houses, Jacuzzis, ski weekends in Vail or Aspen or Telluride, where I learned to yield to wealth. It meant driving the back roads, so fucked up on real, tarry opium, I had my forehead resting on the steering wheel. And it meant pills of every shape, size, and color.

My father's interest in me was spotty. He traveled half the month for work and insisted I take care of myself. He also insisted—to anyone who questioned his method—that I was fucked up because of my overbearing, controlling mother, and I had to be treated as an adult. If teachers, or friends' parents, called with concerns, the story was that I was deeply "troubled" and not to be believed. In that way, everything in the house was a secret, which I had to keep if I wanted all this appalling freedom.

I called him by his first name, cursed freely, had boys— and once a man eight years my senior—sleep over. I crashed a car. When I asked him about the drug use that hung over my childhood, the one my aunt told me about at the Katella Deli, he shrugged it off. He told me my mother, aunt, and he drove around LA with a "silver spoon," which I didn't completely understand or believe (the thought of my aunt doing drugs makes me laugh out loud and is completely untrue). The silver spoon? *A coke spoon,* he explained, an artifact of the seventies, way over my head.

I had even less supervision after my aunt Wendy moved out of his house, a separation I never received an explanation about, though I assumed it must have been my fault.

I bought my own tampons, shampoo, Chinese takeout for dinner. I didn't have to ask if I wanted my own gin and tonic after I made his. When I complained of cramps, he shook his head, not wanting to hear more, and gave me a pill. I remember one night in particular because it was winter, and I was on the screened porch with a space heater, watching—yet again—*The Sound of Music*. I remember it because I had the writerly thought that when the pill hit me, warm butter was being poured over my shoulders, and I stopped shivering. Eventually I didn't have to ask for his Vicodin, Percocet, OxyContin, Ambien, Valium, or the marijuana he kept in his hiking boot.

I never once thought he was an addict. Maybe an alcoholic, but that judgment is relative to the people you spend time with. From him I inherited the belief that it was pedestrian to have one's consumption render one out of control. He was too capable. We threw gorgeous parties at our friend's lake, where my father built bonfires the size of buildings. He showed up to most of my half brother's sports games. He insisted—emphatically—that I never sit down to eat at the table without lighting the candles in Baccarat crystal candleholders, even if I was eating a burrito wrapped in foil, alone. When he was home from his professional traveling, we sat in front of the fireplace together, him reading the paper or *Men's Fitness*, me reading Camus. It wasn't so hard, bonding with him against my mother, wanting to believe that he had been out here the whole time, waiting for me to escape her. I believed that after he'd ignored me for almost my entire life, this was the way it should have been all along.

Washington, D.C.

With margaritas in Styrofoam cups the Monster and I walked in a park where every tree was budding, or already showing cherry blossoms, and he asked, *Would you rather have the Love or the Life?*

It was our first spring. With him, I practiced stoicism so unnatural it bent me in half. All to avoid his looking at me and thinking, *She's hysterical.* I wanted him to admire how different I was from other women, those who would crack under the stress of the situation. Those poor women who wrote love stories and wore their feelings like lace.

Inwardly, a tornado funneled into my stomach. Already I woke in the mornings dry heaving, then throwing up the slices of apple, the cheese plates, the oysters, the banquet of my success, waiting for him to text, waiting for his next visit. Holding perfectly still so he could find me whenever he wanted to. Then I fell into bed at midnight, mind frayed, drugging myself to sleep.

But when he asked me that, I sipped hard through my straw, reminded myself that life was short and I was already close to death, smiled, and whispered in his ear, *I want both.*

His was a rare brand of cynicism that only allowed room for

one feeling at a time. That's why he loved lists, categorizing, ranking, statistics. People like that can compartmentalize like no others, and maybe even enjoy keeping everything separate. I got the Love. His wife got the Life. He could live like that. Maybe he thought it was better that way. He didn't seem to hear me, so I said again, *I thought we were talking about both.*

———

I had a flight to catch, and he wouldn't let me go. We finished lunch at a restaurant near his temporary office, and instead of going back to work he followed me to the bathroom, waited right outside the door. He had packed me a bag of snacks for the plane: carrot sticks and hummus, cheese crisps. I was touched.

His touches were heavy, the small of my back as I went up the stairs, his looks were heavy, wanting to hold me in place. Rare was the time that we parted from each other without panic that it would be the last time. (*Will you come back?* he asked. Or from me: *Tell me the day you are leaving and I will come.* An infinite loop.)

Always the threat that I would have had enough. We—strangely—never thought that he might end things with me. Over and over I said, *If you want to stay married, stop coming for me. It's simple.* Yes, he might never leave her, but he would never stop pursuing me, believing that we had a future. I think he hoped that if he waited long enough, it would take care of itself. *I can't do it unless I know you're there,* he said. *I'm right here,* I said, texting him from a different city. *No,* he said, *I need you here.* I thought he was treading water when he said this. It didn't occur to me that he was really saying, *I don't trust you.*

He trailed my suitcase to the sidewalk, the day turning grizzled during our lunch. Did he notice things like that? I loved to talk about the weather, I always needed to exclaim about the heat, the flakes of snow. *You're so affected by things*, he said, and I didn't know if he meant it kindly. All I meant was that seasons were changing, and I was still with him. The passage of time was supposed to add up to something better. We were still doing this.

It got so gray, I said, eyes up the street, ostensibly searching for a cab but also navigating our private world and the public one.

Yes, it's gray, he said, like I was a child.

It's going to rain, I said, *the air is thick with it. Sigh. Spring.*

Maybe you should stay, he said.

Maybe you should leave, I said. A cab in the distance. I shot my hand up out of instinct, then brought it down out of fear, then put it up again, with force.

We hugged. That part of town was too central for kissing, and we liked that, didn't we? We liked the way the unsaid alerted our bodies, how our desire overcast the days.

Maybe, someday, soon, I said, which is how I always left him. He followed me into the cab, sat next to me. I looked at the driver, scared. *What are you doing? Don't you have to be back at work?*

He shut the door. Told the driver to go to the airport and I started laughing. He put his arm around me. I crawled into his lap. It started to pour rain, a gray smear on the windows. It took us two hours to get to the airport.

Two extra unsupervised hours: tell me you've ever been happier.

I dream about his wife constantly. Sometimes he's there, but more often the two of us are alone.

The Monster wasn't supposed to be married. There was never any prospect I would be a long-term mistress, that we were European, or independently minded people. We were the great loves of each other's lives. It's hard to remember that I wasn't looking for this, because that means he drew me into this to hurt me. Regardless, the punitive nature feels correct, every hurt deserved.

I long for his wife. Sometimes I hate her, or pity her, but mostly my longing is for contact. Forgiveness. One night in a dream she corners me at a wedding. She has a small bandage on her face in this dream, and when I spy her in the crowd, I am filled with pity at the sight of the bandage. She says, *What happened with you and my husband, all those years ago?*

In the dream, I want to reach for her, fix her bandage, offer her some lipstick. In the dream, I am exhausted, should be put to bed. I want to say, *We have so much in common, don't we?* I think back—in the dream—to this affair, which—in the dream—has passed—and I tell her the truth: *Nothing actually happened. It was a lot of talk, but I swear to you, nothing happened.*

In the dream I feel peace about the affair. I'm grateful to her for taking the burden of loving him. Upon waking that relief is spread over me like a weighted blanket, I can't move. For a second, it's finally over.

———

One day the Monster says, *Your pills worry me.* My face burns like I've been slapped.

I'll come out of it, I say. *I always do.*

It doesn't seem to occur to him that my "pills" and I have arrived at this point in no small part due to the fucking roller coaster he's put me on. Another winter morning in the canyon, threads of ice in the corners of my window, I wake up alone, check the weather in New York, and realize it's been months since I had a night's sleep that wasn't benzodiazepine-assisted.

Like most people alive, I'm interested in presence. In escaping the feeling of time, an infinite substance loaned to us in shockingly finite amounts. Time, to me, is synonymous with death. Presence cures time. I'm present when in a stage of love called limerence: hyper-alert, the world hallucinatory, my limbs jumping as if they had been asleep for years. I am my best, most observant self. I'm present when I orgasm. I become thoughtless, language-less, if only for a moment or two. I've achieved, only a few times, a drowsy buzz while meditating that falls into this category as well.

But the quickest way to get there is drugs, with which I have an understandably complicated relationship. As a child, I was terrified by them, ever since my aunt took me to that fateful Katella Deli dinner and explained that cocaine was the reason I didn't have a father. I was never scared of dying from drugs. Instead my fear was that if I did drugs, I would hurt the people I loved.

I'm also blessed with an extremely sensitive stomach. I'm not physically built for drugs or any binge behavior. I was an anxious child, anxious teenager, anxious adult. Pot was the first thing available, but it was too heady. I didn't know how to drink either. I gagged constantly. The first time I pounded a beer, I threw up. I still can't take a shot, or I'll vomit on the bar. The first time I took a drag of a cigarette, I threw up. Every time I took a pill of ecstasy—and I've taken plenty—I threw up right before my pupils blew out and my eyeballs started shaking like loose marbles. Every time I waited for acid to hit, I threw up. The first time I snorted opioids I vomited—the most pleasurable vomiting of my life—for four hours.

It's not just the first time. This remains true. And yet, I've persisted, right on the edge. I'm attracted to my limits, but I never had the desire to transcend them. And while I am not painting a picture of health, neither am I painting a picture of someone who lusts after high-risk behavior. And while I do linger close to an edge that experience tells me can be catastrophic, nothing I imbibe, from a beer to a vitamin, is thoughtless. Still this habit of needing help sleeping reminds me of two times in my life I've identified a problem.

When I got to New York City in 2006, cocaine fixed my drinking problem (my "problem" being not being able to drink for long stretches). One drink, one bump, and so on, and I could keep up after-hours with the chefs and sommeliers I worshipped. I loved not getting drunk. I loved being articulate, startling myself with insight. I started buying my own, and then I was nearly always in possession of a bag.

And then during the last year of my marriage, my ex-husband and I drank like the professionals we purported to be. We had one day off from work together a week. Negronis—plural—accompanied our oyster happy hour at four p.m. Then a bottle of white wine, then a bottle of red. Often a third bottle was opened. Then I sipped oloroso sherry as we wound down for bed, and he finished every single night with a glass, or glasses, of bourbon. This, for us, was a quiet day. When our marriage dissolved—for seemingly unrelated reasons, though I couldn't have asked for a clearer symptom that we were in trouble—I was left with my tolerance, but no drinking buddy. I couldn't stop. I started to keep a diary of my intake. What followed was a year where I didn't go a single day without a drink. Occasionally it would be just one. Very occasionally. I would look at myself in the mirror and think, *This doesn't end well.*

Xanax, generally, is perfect for me. When I stopped being able to fly without sweating, crying, and (you guessed it) throwing up, I got a prescription. I still had to break up the pills into tiny doses (I am a small person), but even a quarter of .5 milligrams helped me achieve real sleep. It didn't erase my anxiety, but absorbed it, like an extra barrier, like carrying within me the prescribed Buddhist "pause" between action and reaction. But Xanax isn't "fun." I can't drink with it or I'll pass out. Recreationally, it's great for vacuuming and watching reruns of *Sex and the City*. And it was fine for panic attacks, the real ones, which I've weathered since I was a child, which have begun in earnest again now. When I drive back from my mother's, my wrists seize up, fingertips numb. I bang them against the steering wheel to get the feeling back.

In the past, I just stopped. The mania ran its course. I didn't have to pray. The first time I went a week without alcohol it was nearly accidental. I couldn't stop laughing about it. But here in Laurel Canyon, I feel that these broken bits of pills are buffering me from some more serious crisis, like it's one of the last stakes keeping me in place. I don't know. For so long I've been fighting my way toward what I imagine is light, but I'm beginning to wonder what's on the other side of this.

Laurel Canyon, California

It sounds like rain on a cloudless day, a needling, then persistent tapping. It moves faster against the wall in my study. I look up and the Laurel Canyon hillside is coming down, dirt, uprooted agaves, and the boulders that made up part of a retaining wall. As the boulders roll toward the window, I think, *Oh, fuck*.

I yell and they drop like thunder against the house. When things are still again, I go outside, peering up at the cliff above the cottage. I see the line of eucalyptus trees. Some of the roots are now exposed where the hillside has fallen away. *Oh, fuck*. The trees seem to sway.

Those eucalyptuses, four of them, are completely dead, which is why their root systems aren't holding the hillside in place. This I was told by a professional. My landlord says it sounds like *a little debris*, even when I send him photos of the entire section of wall that crashed against the house. I end up stopping a tree guy on my way home from the Country Store. He comes over to give me an estimate. *Twenty thousand*, he says. Five k for each tree. And he can't even take the job for a month.

The canyon keeps me in business. Drives me crazy though. It's fucking impossible to get equipment up here. I'm reminded of what the fire chief said about the fires. The tree guy whistles looking up at the ridge. *It's not if, but when.*

I end up watching a "Classic Albums" documentary on Fleetwood Mac's *Rumours*. At minute twenty-two, the camera reveals a black-and-white photograph of Christine and John McVie. They're standing in my front window, which is the size of double doors and swings completely open. I get the chills, then start laughing. I'm alone but my bed feels crowded with ghosts. I wonder if they worried about the eucalyptus, about the houses built on stilts on top of them. I know Stevie did. People think Stevie Nicks wrote "Landslide" about her father. She actually wrote it during her first snowy winter in Aspen, before Mick Fleetwood called, when she was cleaning houses to support her and Lindsey Buckingham's musical aspirations. Lindsey had left her to tour. She was alone and miserable, waiting for him to come home, wondering if she screamed would it cause an avalanche.

Carly insists I talk to her psychic. Visiting my mother, this push/pull of the Monster, the constant countdown until a decisive, exploded moment, has undermined my ability to be certain about anything. I miss all my turns. I don't know how to grocery shop—I lose my cart, come out with nothing I needed and things that make no sense: three different kombuchas, some cheese, no crackers.

I'm falling apart, I write the Monster. *Please help me.* He calls me dutifully and is silent. *Say something.*

I need more time.

This psychic has been in Carly's life for years and accurately predicted major life events, like her second pregnancy. I've never trusted these telepathic types, and the idea of healing makes me cringe. I have a therapist, and when I tell her about the psychic, she stifles a laugh. And yet, I can't stop crying the week I finally call Carly's psychic. In the shower, in the car, running into the bathroom at coffee shops, at Carly's house, crying. So why not?

As I Skype in, I remember that I have seen a fortune-teller once before, when I was seventeen. On a boat, in Greece, outside Santorini. He was the captain and wore a turban that I'm thinking now might have been a costume. He said he saw a dark mark on me. He led me away from the group. He rubbed my palm and said that I had dreams but I would never achieve them the way I was going. Which, looking back, was true. He added at the last minute that I wouldn't marry my true love. Which I haven't thought of in over a decade and is a fucked-up thing to tell a girl.

All I want to discuss is the Monster, but I want this psychic to read me. I feign nonchalance. Tell her there is *nothing special* that brought me to her.

She says I am a conduit. I download massive amounts of information from the metaphysical realm.

I'm a writer, I say. She responds with a smug smile.

She sees me with a backpack. *Maybe hiking,* I say. I do walk a lot. *I've walked all over the world, I even did a pilgrimage trail across Spain.* She considers me.

It was forty-three days of walking, I explain, as if that were crucial.

Or it could be your baggage, she says. *It appears to be a very heavy backpack. Your pain body that you carry with you at all times.*

Right, I say, thinking to myself, *it's not literal backpacking, you fucking moron.*

When I try to bring up the Monster, she's bored. I'm careful about it. I say, *I'm in a . . . well . . . it's kind of . . . a bad thing . . .*

. . . With an unavailable man. I see it now. He is a shadow of you. In the shadow is everything you fear. He's not real. You created him and you can free yourself from him.

Okay, I say. *Well. He is real. Technically. And I think he's my . . . I don't know, soul mate. I'm pretty sure that the rest of my life will be determined by whether or not he and I can get our shit together and love each other.*

No, she says. *I don't see you with him.*

A pause flies up between us. I wait for her to continue. She doesn't.

So. You just don't see me with him.

She shakes her head. *He is a shadow. You are the light.* She leans in closer to the screen. *I do see you pregnant though. Are you pregnant?*

Um. Not really.

Is there a possibility that you could become pregnant?

Not really.

Maybe you have something big coming in the spring? I can see that you're full, and about to give birth.

A book, I say, annoyed. Duh, the fucking book.

The book is going to be a success, she says, smiling. I mimic her smile.

I'm not sure I believe that, I say. Did I really Venmo a stranger in the Valley to tell me this?

She stares at me through the computer. She squints.

You disbelieve a lot. I see that you don't believe in angels.

No. I don't. I sigh. *How could you tell?*

The psychic sits back, satisfied. *The angel sitting behind you just told me.*

The Love Interest hands me white sage. Black sage. Yerba santa. California bay leaves. He points to the burned-out trees and references the fires that blackened them, he notices the way the foliage clings to the cliffsides in the micro canyons as we climb. He waves his hand at the view below us, understanding the layout of the roads, housing developments, as a function of topography, not the personal whims I imagined dictated this place. At the end of the day, I take off the flannel I've been wearing, and these crushed green things fall out of my pocket. I press them into my notebooks.

"Stephanie," the Love Interest says from the other room of the cottage. My heart swells and I'm mortified. *What is wrong with me?* I keep asking. I've lost all sense of proportion. How brutal is my other relationship that a man addressing me kindly by my full name makes me want to cry?

As the Love Interest asks me to walk through California, these mountains I never knew, the muscle memory kicks in of walking with my father. When I can build a fire, get a car unstuck from an ice patch, or when I know to lock the food in the car when we camp, the Love Interest asks where I learned this stuff. *My dad*, I say, *how about you? Did you camp as a child?* Deflecting questions with other questions is waitressing 101.

My father would be up at five a.m., blasting the classic rock station throughout the house, and I would moan, knowing that meant we were hiking. We ranged through Rocky Mountain National Park, up to glacier lakes, skirting the tree line, glimpsing bears, leaning into a quiet that I've never found again in my adult life. After my divorce, I walked across Spain and thought, this was his gift to me, this cure. I don't look anything like my father, but when I walk, I'm his daughter.

It occurs to me that the Love Interest would have enjoyed him. The way he used to be.

If I was a different person, I would tell the Love Interest that when it was just the three of us in the house, my mother and her girls, we never put on clothes and we danced all evening. We huddled together every morning and said, *Yay team!* before leaving the house to do battle in the world. We bathed together, singing songs my mother made up. She had a beautiful alto singing voice. I have a record of her singing "Fever" with her high school band that I would listen to obsessively, on repeat, before begging her to sing it again for us.

When my father taught me to drive a stick, he let me throw the clutch out excessively and he laughed. That was a time he was patient. When he came home from those work trips, I hugged him, and I knew he had missed me. He would chase me with lobsters, or dead, iridescently plumed pheasants he shot, and I would jump and run. We could pass time silently in the mountains and I felt understood by him.

All I say is: *I did not erase the good to punish them. I erased it because it hurts me.*

———

Back in the early 1900s when my cottage was a hunting cottage connected to the trails, the Laurel Canyon Country Store was a lodge for the deer hunters that saturated these hills. It's still a refuge in a community that feels commercially isolated, though Sunset Boulevard and West Hollywood are technically a minute away. My writing days revolve around the Country Store. I walk there in the morning for coffee at Lily's cart, another walk in the early evening for whatever pantry supply or mediocre bottle of Pinot Grigio I'm in desperate need of. The Los Angeles cliché notwithstanding, with the mood I'm in I haven't used a car in a while.

I don't know where these people come from who hang out at the Country Store all day, from the time I get my coffee in the morning to the time I come back in the late afternoon. They are all older than fifty, wearing the same outfits day to day. They look like people who live in their cars. They have nicknames for each other. They've lived in the canyon for ages. Hippies that time forgot, buffered from having to create income by some lucky scheme or real estate break.

Lily, who runs the coffee cart, is nice enough to me, but doesn't remember my order from one day to the next. I'm not her people. I'm too reticent and buttoned up. My clothes were bought new. My decade back East has wired my brain against these drifters and burnouts, and I ask myself, *Why doesn't anyone work?* But then, what am I doing here? I'm struggling with the idea that I could work by writing. Everyone on the patio looks so at ease, I want whatever drugs they're on. I reason that they are calmer because they probably don't have smartphones.

As I'm leaving, Sam waves me over. He's "a doctor," "an analyst," "a playwright," "a movie producer," and an asshole. Though he's in his sixties, and not attractive, he's decided that he's going to date me. Thus he's my only friend at the Country Store. When I sit with him, he asks me how it's going, but before I can answer he's regaling me with exaggerated stories or just lies, waxing on about the fifteen acres he owns up near Mulholland (I'm not sure there are fifteen free acres in these hills, but I let it go). He's building an artists' retreat there. He'll let me apply to participate in the inaugural group. There will be a sign at the gate that says *ALL MEN OF REASON MAY ENTER HERE.* *It's John Stuart Mill,* he says (it's not), and he says with a wink, *All the women have to use another entrance.* He also once told me that *women are just horny little bitches,* and that Margaret Mead invited him to lecture at Columbia, but all she wanted to do was fuck.

The Love Interest hates him, based on the two times they met when we walked up to Lily's for breakfast. And I don't know why I humor Sam, or do I? He's obviously unbalanced, manic, and a grotesque misogynist. Still I get sucked into his rants, nodding, thanking him for unsolicited advice, placating him. He's always surrounded by a group of pals, making me feel as if I'm the cer- tifiably insane one. He brought me a bound copy of his one-man play with two roles: the actor—himself presumably—will play MAN and MAN'S EGO who fight to the death. I read two pages and it was, indeed, terrible, despite Sam being *one of the lead- ing experts in the world* on Freud. He says he's able to make art because he once assisted the former Shah of Iran on a thirteen- billion-dollar deal, and he lives off the generated interest. One day he tells me there's *an epidemic of women in the streets, women way past their prime that still think they're hot shit,* and he looks me up and down.

It becomes clear, when he claps for himself after he recites a poem that he wrote *on the spot* and then sang for me, that I'm nice to him because bits of him remind me of my parents. In his monologues I've learned he has a daughter who won't speak to him (shocking) and though he thinks he wants to fuck me, I know that with whatever antipsychotics he favors, he hasn't had an erection in a decade. I sit with him because I find his loneliness so familiar. He never asks what I do, and that's all right because I wouldn't know how to answer that anyway.

Nowhere

The first disappearance came when I was three. The original marker in my ongoing, never-ending anxiety about safety.

The scattered, inconsistent, and infrequent visitations. The times he was supposed to have one but canceled at the last second, my mother furious, but also vindicated.

Every time, on one of those rare visits, that he took the money my mother had given us for candy and bought a six-pack of beer to finish on the drive from Long Beach to San Pedro, I would be certain, my arm across my sister like an extra seat belt, that he'd forgotten he had children.

Coming back from a class trip to Greece, one of the many outlandish features of this private high school, I got really sick on the plane. A fever, a rash, vomiting most of the flight home. All of the parents waited at the gate, excited to have their children home, hear their stories. He wasn't at the airport. He didn't answer his phone. My best friend's mother insisted I come home with them, where she nursed me, and I slept for two days without leaving the guest room. He eventually came and got me. He said I had told him the wrong date.

There were countless times at the Hygiene house when I wouldn't know he was gone for work. I'd wake in the morning and notice his un-mussed sheets. If I texted him, he was usually in China. One time stands out because it was winter, and he had taken my car and left me his truck—which had no heat. He had also forgotten to leave the house key where we usually hid it. I got home from my shift at the café and had to sleep in the truck inside the garage, returning to school the next day in the same clothes, raising alarm in my teachers. I stayed with my best friend the rest of the week. He finally texted me that he had been in Japan. He was angry that I hadn't watered the houseplants.

Another time he was dropping me off for my junior-year semester abroad in Rome and his gout flared up on the plane. When we landed, his ankle was elephantine and he could barely walk. He made me go from pharmacy to pharmacy begging for Vicodin in a language I didn't speak or understand. He bought a cane, limped around. We ate with Carly—who would be my roommate in Rome—and her mother. My father skipped out on the bill for lunch. He went out for a smoke and didn't come back. Carly's mom said, knowingly, *Your dad's an alcoholic, right?*

Two days later I came downstairs early for breakfast and he was at the front desk with his suitcases and the walking cane, checking out. He was needed in Switzerland immediately, he told me. He left and hadn't paid for my room.

Though he flew in to see my mother when she was in a coma at Long Beach Memorial hospital, he left within forty-eight hours. I'm not sure if we exchanged a word, but I remember hugging him and being glad he came. His appearance of health made him seem stable.

The way my father sold a story, these absences were only signs of his importance in the world. A god on loan from Olympus. Then came our cross-country drive to my senior year of college. But that was already at the end of this story and the beginning of the next.

Hygiene, Colorado

The Hygiene house pulsed red on the humid August night that I pulled into the driveway after sixteen hours straight through from Los Angeles. Three years earlier, for my freshman year of college, my father and I had driven from Colorado to Ohio. We'd had fun, stopped in St. Louis and had a big steakhouse dinner. He got a distinct pride from my university, Kenyon, modeled on Oxford, where he had gone himself.

We were repeating that drive for my senior year. That morning I had left California with my sister crying and my mother in the hands of the nurse. My sister's tears: I didn't know until I started driving that I was abandoning her. But I knew it every hour I got farther from California: I wasn't ever going back. I would keep going east. After I graduated, I was going to live in New York City.

I hadn't seen my father since Nancy's coma, and before that, since his odd disappearance in Rome. After an emotionally draining summer, watching my mother advance, then regress, listening to her murmur that she wanted to die while I sat with her in the sun, watching her dive headfirst back into the tequila she had hidden under the kitchen sink, I was looking forward to being with him.

Red light was the heat lamps he left on in the kitchen, and yellow light came from his bedroom. It was past midnight, and I was surprised he was still awake. When I turned off the car, there was only the hum of mosquitos and the cows' mournful callings, that Colorado symphony.

I came into the house, which reeked of cigarette smoke, never a habit of my father's. The floors creaked upstairs where I could hear him walking. I called out, *Stephen, I'm here.*

Sweetheart. I'm just finishing up some work.

My father had been laid off in the spring, the story convoluted, but I had been in Rome and I hadn't asked any questions in the middle of my mother's coma. I wondered what work he was doing. Maybe he had already found a job. I turned off the red lights in the kitchen. The fridge was jarringly empty. I crouched to a cupboard, found a Clif bar I had left four years ago, and ate it as I climbed the stairs.

That red light makes it look like The Shining *in here . . .*

I stopped mid-step and mid-sentence. My father stood in front of me, his arms open, waiting for me to embrace him. Except the man in front of me didn't look like my father. He was half his weight. His boxers and T-shirt hung off of him. His head a large stone, precariously balanced. He held a cigarette in one hand.

Wow.

How was the drive?

Stephen, you . . . You lost a lot of weight.

He was running. Five days a week (*But your knees . . . you've never been able to run*). That was the yoga, of course. His instructor was a cute blonde, just his type, unsurprisingly. They were going to do Longs Peak, I remembered climbing Longs Peak with him, didn't I?

I did remember. I hugged him, tired.

He was also cutting back on the drinking. The weight just fell off. The smoking helped him not drink. Very French, right? He hadn't had gout in years (*You just had it in Rome. In January*). He laughed. God, he had forgotten about that. Did I remember those elephant ankles in Rome, wasn't that hilarious?

I did. I moved toward my old room. *I'm exhausted.*

Everything in my room was in boxes. My father was selling the house and "moving to town," which meant twenty minutes away in Boulder. He told me if I didn't get my stuff out he was going to throw it away, but I didn't know how much of this I could take back to my apartment at Kenyon.

You remember this old place?

I shrugged. Touched the sheets, expected to feel more, but those boxes made my life in Colorado recede. It was that room in which I wrote so many angsty stories and poems, where bats flew in the screenless windows and made me scream. Tonight it felt like none of that actually happened.

My father didn't want to sell the house, but it was tough times. He wanted to finally finish the pool, but this would help, this would bridge the gap between jobs, plus he was a bachelor again. He wanted to be able to walk to the coffee shop, be out on the town, mingle. But he did love this house. He might buy it back. Did I remember those Fourth of July parties where he shot off the illegal fireworks and the neighbors called the cops? He had to bring those fireworks in from Nebraska. We, his kids, had loved them, did I remember?

I did. *Can you not smoke in here? It makes me sick.*

When he swerved leaving the room to extinguish the cigarette, I thought he was pretty drunk. I changed quickly for sleep from the backpack I brought in. He was back in my doorway in what felt like seconds, holding a large stack of yellow legal pads.

This lawsuit is really heating up. He gestured to the legal pads and sat at the edge of my bed.

Oh, he couldn't say too much about it, but there were dirty dealings, and he was at the top. Seventeen years at the company. He knew too much. They laid him off, but now he was the whistle-blower on this whole case, and though he'd been advised not to talk about it, he could talk to me about it because I was his daughter, he was looking at clearing . . . millions.

Wow. I sat on my bed. *So I'm super tired. I had to leave Nancy this morning. And we leave early in the morning—*

About the morning. Did I remember Donna?

Do I remember your girlfriend of five years who I desperately wanted you to marry? Who was way too good for you? And I cried for a week when you guys broke up? Yeah I remember her.

Donna still loved him. That's the truth. He had seen her recently and she was asking about me. He told her all about me, my prestigious university, how I was moving to New York after I graduated. He also took that opportunity to tell Donna that she was the only woman he had ever loved.

Stephen, I said quietly. Now I thought he must be very drunk. *You guys broke up years ago.*

He corrected me. He had lost track of Donna but imagined it was more a "break" than "breakup." She didn't want any contact, at least that's what she said, but *you know women, they don't say what they mean.* Anyway, he found her. He had been having his ex-wife Kelly followed, and he used the same guy, a private investigator (*Are you joking?*) and a former aerospace guy, like himself, anyway, this guy helped my father find out where Donna was working, and found out that she was engaged. *Engaged!* My father was insulted. So he decided to surprise her at her office, he waited for her at her car, and *boy was she surprised*. He looked great, at his fighting weight, and she was thrilled to see him. This was when she asked about me. But he had other news for her, some dirt on her new fiancé. They shared a doctor in Boulder, the best guy in Boulder, Donna's fiancé and my father. My father had flirted a little with the doctor's secretary, he took the woman out to dinner a few times, slept with her (*What?*). I knew how it all worked, didn't I? Well this secretary pulled this guy's file for my father, the fiancé's file. And now my father had to tell her the truth, didn't he? Wasn't that the only thing to do?

Vasectomy! my father declared. He started laughing. *Can you believe that?*

I looked at my father, closely, in the light, for the first time since I had arrived.

What happened to your skin? I whispered. My father's neck, up to his cheek and into his scalp, was dotted with swollen red lumps, some of them broken and scabbed, other larger patches scaly and flaking.

Hives, he said. He sighed. *I'm on steroids to clear them up, but it's reacting badly with my skin.*

I moved closer. *You're picking the hives?*

They itch, he said, covering one with his hand.

I can put some calamine on them. Will that help?

I kept my eyes averted from the mirror in the bathroom where I found the calamine. Everything seemed to be in its place: there were essential oils I had used in the bath in high school. Nail clippers where they used to be. I noticed my hands were shaking. *Maybe*, I thought to myself, *I'm overtired from the drive*. I had that familiar dissociation, where I felt far from the house, outside my

body. I came back into the room and sat behind him as he looked
at a legal pad, covered from first to last page with his own writing. I counted seven of them.

You take good care of me, he said, his voice calmer. *We had a
good time, didn't we?*

I nodded. As I worked on one sore, he reached up and scratched
another. A scab popped off and a small burst of blood snaked into
the pink lotion. I bit my lip. I quieted my breathing and used the
voice I used on my mom in the hospital.

*We did have a good time. We were like two bachelors living out
here. We had some nice walks, some great parties. We did all right.*

I plastered my father's neck and temples in pink lotion. I blew
on it to dry. He was motionless for the first time since I had
walked up the stairs. The scab he had picked was still bleeding,
the blood about to hit his shirt collar. I told him I had to grab a
tissue and his body recoiled. He left and returned to my room
holding tissues to his neck, smearing the pink.

Donna, it turns out, was shocked that her fiancé had had
a vasectomy. He was promising her kids. *Shocked.* A massive
betrayal. My father then mentioned to her that I was coming
through town in a few weeks, and well, she very much wanted to
see me. She wanted some alone time with me, but he's thinking
that she and I could get some breakfast tomorrow and he could
pop in at the end. Surprise her again. What did I think?

No, I said.

You could do a favor for your father. His voice hardened. I knew
what was coming. He could be cruel when he was drinking.

*After all the bullshit I've put up with from you. After I saved your
life. You'd be dead if I hadn't rescued you from your mother. The for-
tune I've spent on you. Cleaned up all your messes. How do you think
you got into college? You can't possibly think you deserve to be there?*

Whose money was bailing you out? You can't do a simple favor for your father?

I can't, Stephen. I surprised myself by wanting to cry even though I had heard this entire rant many times before. *I think you're drunk.*

He didn't hear me. He was spinning through his pages. There, there it was. He had been writing Donna poems. Did I remember that he had studied poetry? He loved Chaucer. He had wanted to be a writer too; did I remember that? He wasn't spoiled though, not like me. He had to work.

I work, I said, barely whispering. He held some pages aloft and started reading:

Tonight, I can write the saddest lines . . .

Pablo Neruda, I thought. *He thinks he wrote a Pablo Neruda poem.* I listened to him read it all the way through.

I told him that Donna would love it and maybe I could have a call with her if it meant that much to him. I asked him if I could borrow an Ambien and when he went to his bathroom, I went downstairs, keeping the lights off. When I hit the bottom stair, I stepped again, and I stepped again. I looked to the cupboards for help. *What is happening?* I put on water for tea. I made two cups of mint tea and went back up the stairs and tried to make myself thoughtless. There was fear but no cognition. I thought maybe on top of the drinking he had mixed pills that shouldn't be mixed. I understood that his behavior was the result of something chemical gone wrong, but I didn't have the courage—the strength?—to speculate. When I thought about calling someone, I couldn't think of whom to call.

I came back into my room, and my father was lying in my teenage bed, all the lights on, the sheets thrown off. His legal pads stacked next to him. He rested against the pillows and seemed to be asleep. There were two pills on the nightstand. I replaced them with a cup of tea for him and sat down on the floor. He snored lightly. I burned my mouth on the tea and took another sip, tonguing the immediate blister on the roof of my mouth. I noticed that my father's legs had the hives as well. I noticed that his testicles had fallen out of his boxers, making him as naked and vulnerable as I've ever seen him.

And still, I wanted nothing but to get back to school. I wanted to excise the memory of nursing my mother, to believe that one of my parents was okay. I was so focused on surviving, I did not think about my safety. My father and I started our drive the next morning at six a.m., and I pretended the night before hadn't happened. Forgetting, for me, was the equivalent of loving.

I can recall with harrowing clarity images of that drive to my senior year of college. What I cannot recall is how I felt beyond the fear, and even that is fuzzy. Here's what I know:

His knees bounced like a marionette's while he used them to pilot the car, his hands fanning the pages of his attaché case, open on his lap.

His cell phone never stopped ringing.

Something was wrong with the sale of the house. Someone had fucked him over. He needed the sale to close.

We stopped for him to use the bathroom every two hours, sometimes every hour.

He had two realtors working on the sale of the house. They didn't know about each other, until they did. I listened to him berate one woman, only to jump on the phone with the other and call her *a fucking moron*.

He threw a half-full water bottle at my face because I had interrupted his phone call by asking him to pull over because he was scaring me.

He was sick in the bathroom of a gas station in Kansas.

He said it was the steroids, or an illness, maybe a stomach bug. I suggested he see the doctor as soon as we got to campus.

He was still yelling into his phone, attaché case still open in his lap, when he swerved onto the grassy center median and swerved back onto the highway.

I screamed at him, pounded the windows, the dashboard with my hands, demanded he pull over. He let me drive after that. He broke up bits of Ambien in front of me and slept, a hulking adult, tangled in his seat belt, mouth wide open.

We stopped in St. Louis but there was no steak dinner. We checked into a Hilton in the middle of the afternoon. He drew the blackout blinds and crawled into bed while I read in the bath. I ate a vending machine bag of Doritos for dinner.

He checked into the Kenyon Inn on campus and said he would see me in the morning. We were supposed to go to Walmart to pick out a lamp and some sheets for my apartment. He promised he would see the doctor. I went to get him the next morning and he was gone.

I had the presence of mind to call my cousin James. My ex-stepmother, Kelly. I said he was having a mental breakdown. That he seemed dangerously disconnected from reality. They said they would keep an eye on it.

And still, I didn't have a vocabulary for what was happening. I didn't know how to explain anything to my boyfriend, my friends. I glossed over it with a joke, *You know my dad.* Carly's mother bought me sheets.

Hygiene, Colorado

The first time I can remember spending more than a few minutes with both of my parents in the same room was my high school graduation. My father—ever a showman—threw a massive party at our house in Hygiene. There were apple blossoms all over the lawn and cherries in the trees, all the drenched colors of late spring. My best friend in Colorado came into the house and raised her eyebrows, saying, *Look at all this family you have!* After knowing me for two years, she thought of me as parentless: estranged from my mother, and with a father, whom she saw sometimes, hardly more than a specter.

I know, I said, surveying them. *They love a party.*

My mother and I were tensely polite. I could be magnanimous because I had won. She had tried to punish me, and look at this place: the rust-colored foothills, evenings that flew with the geese, the delicate air. I had absorbed my father's superiority. I learned from him to call Los Angeles *an intellectual backwater.* I watched her and my aunt take in the derelict hippies on Pearl Street, the co-op markets, the athleisure wear, with barely contained disgust. I thought them snobs. *You guys should go on a hike*, I told my mom with a straight face, and my sister and I laughed through our noses.

What do you think will happen, Christina and I asked each other, *when our parents have to spend an evening together?* We put money on both of them getting drunk, our father trying to tease our mother, or worse, trying to tease our aunt, who might or might not actually murder him regardless of witnesses. Our mother would become grim and say something nasty. She was, after all, *so bitter*, and *such a bitch*. Christina and I were fortressed off from feeling. What else could we do?

At the party, my father lifted up his gin-and-tonic tumbler and chimed it with a fork. I rolled my eyes at my sister. This man loved giving a fucking speech. He had written a poem, one that teased me and congratulated himself for surviving me. He laughed at his own jokes about my destructiveness. But after the poem he became serious. He looked around the crowded room and said that he wasn't sure this day would come. Two years ago, living in California, my prospects had been bleak. He realized he had a role to play: that he could take me in—as he had taken in other strays in the family—and help me turn my life around. He knew he had to save me. *Now look at her. Off to Kenyon College. She's going to be a writer!*

Everyone in the room turned and looked at me. They raised their glasses at me. My mother didn't but most everyone else did. My friend came up to me and sighed. *Your dad's a piece of work.*

What she meant was that I hadn't gotten into college. I graduated from my private high school having been rejected or waitlisted by every university I applied to. Even with my test scores on the SATs and my AP English class, my GPA was garbage. I had failed multiple classes in California and continued to earn average grades in science and math. The rejections included state schools like Colorado State and Long Beach State. The truth is that on the day of this party, I had a job as a barista and an acceptance at the community college in Boulder.

There was, of course, the wait list at Kenyon. A liberal arts school in the middle-of-nothing Ohio—renowned for their writing program—that my high school English teacher had attended. That teacher fought to get me an interview with the dean of admissions. He also got them to accept my short stories, which I wrote prodigiously under his guidance, with my application. God knows how else he begged them, but the credit that evening surely belonged to him. I did secure an interview. The only problem was that my father wouldn't take me. Whether he was busy with work, or simply didn't believe I would get in, he was not available to visit the one college I had a slim chance of obtaining admission to. At the eleventh hour, my father's sister, my aunt Wendy, flew with me to Ohio, drove me to Kenyon. She took one look around the campus and said, *This is where you'll become a writer.*

But that day at my father's party, the letter inviting me to Kenyon was still weeks away from arriving. I was familiar with my father's exaggeration, his *harmless* white lies. The reason this memory haunts me is thinking about my mother listening to this parable of heroism. The way he manipulated me and everyone around him into believing he was a savior, the way he made an outcast of the woman who gave up all of her aspirations to raise me and tried—I know now that she tried—to love me. She had to watch everyone raise a glass to my father, to say behind her back that it really was incredible, what he was able to do with me. *It is no wonder,* my sister says now, *she hated him.*

Laurel Canyon, California

My book went into the Library of Congress today.

Impressive, the Monster says.

And I bought a new computer, I tell him. *I'm going to write another book.*

He's proud of me. But then there's nothing more to say about it, and we write dirty texts about all kinds of fucking.

Yesterday I called my therapist from my parked car on Beverly Boulevard, where I had meant to get lunch, but I couldn't eat, why would I ever eat, because he had done it to me again. Again. It was an anniversary of the affair yesterday and he sent flowers.

The impact of most crashes is immediate, the card read. *This has been much worse. Love, the Monster.*

My book went into the Library of Congress under the category: "Self-Realization in Women."

I text him all the things I would do to his cock that I would never do to his cock. Or I might during his lunch break, or during a layover in the next synthetic place we met, the next carpeted hotel room, somewhere between the first drink when we were hopeful and the last drink when I was yelling at him. The truth is, we mostly fucked facelessly via the Internet.

I've been game to pause my entire life to text with him. I traveled all over the world and was paralyzed in one conversation with one man. When I was in Egypt, on a Nile cruise for a writing assignment, I sat huddled on the floor in pajamas outside the closed captain's office. It was the only place with solid Wi-Fi. I stayed there until two a.m., ignoring other guests walking past me back to their rooms, though I saw them whisper or share a look. At a residency in the Catskills I stood outside a closed office in a snowstorm because it was the only place with service. I've walked into people, trash cans, walls, while texting. I've been almost hit by cars more times than I can count. Twice, I've pulled over onto the shoulder of the freeway. My days are made up of intervals of activity between the deluge of texting that starts when I wake and ends when his wife comes home. But today I am bothered. I need to get in the shower.

He writes that he wants to fuck me from behind with my face shoved into the pillows but that he will pull me back by my hair when I need to breathe. *Maybe*, he writes. *Jesus*, I write back.

I can't shower, return emails, drive, leave my seat, until he finishes jerking off in the bathroom stall at his work.

I'm going to explode, he writes.

Jesus, I write again.

He thinks *Jesus* means, *Fuck I'm so turned on, I'm coming so hard*, but it means, *Jesus, you fucking moron, you think this is romantic?*

I am talking to both of us.

At the same time, my agent, my editor, and I are on a group text.

#selfrealizationinwomen

Lots of champagne-glasses-clinking, heart-eyed emojis. I smack myself in the face as hard as I can and text back: *Yay!*

Once in graduate school I was workshopping pages of a novel in progress and a man—whose prose I very much admired—had his turn to weigh in.

It's good, he said. *It's really good.*

I waited patiently for the "but."

But I hope this isn't going to be just a love story. It's better than that.

I ran up to him after class. *Of course it's not just a love story,* I assured him. Novels are about big ideas: class, gender, race, religion, politics. It definitely had a theme like The American Identity, The Human Condition, The Failure of Language. I thanked him for his appraisal in class, which seemed to imply that if I applied myself, really focused, I might be a serious writer.

It wasn't until days later, as I sat at the table to write, that I thought, *Wait. What is just a love story?*

Los Angeles, California

Up at the top of a hill in the Pacific Palisades is a house with the most jaw-dropping views I've seen in Los Angeles. The Charmel house was built on a northwest-facing cliff overlooking a ravine and Topanga State Park, the mountains of Malibu, and the Pacific Ocean. You can't see another house, or even a road, when you look out. There is nothing ahead of you but green and blue, nothing beneath you but air. When the sun sets, you could easily be in another, less developed country. I like to imagine that this is what California looked like before we got here.

This is Alex's house, or, to be more precise, Alex's parents' house. During breaks from college, if I came back to California, I would bounce between Carly's house in Santa Monica and Alex's house in the Palisades, avoiding Seal Beach, Naples, and my family. Kenyon College was teeming with unmodified wealth, the kind that felt liquid and made the ski homes in Colorado look basic. I was used to visiting my friends' ostentatious homes, also their second and third homes. Used to being taken out on boats, then to a clambake, or noting a Matisse, a row of Rauschenbergs, or a Lucian Freud. And while I never stopped noticing, I did learn to swallow the guttural surprise of seeing art in a private residence and temper my recognition of a house that had been featured in *Architectural Digest*. I grew accustomed to the staff, ever-present. Within that jaded bubble, Charmel was still something spectacular. The house seemed built out of glass, so it decanted light, the swimming pool chopped into the hillside, the air always fragrant with thyme. The closets in this house were bigger than any bedroom I'd had in my life.

This house is full of warm memories for me. The generosity of Alex's mother and father combined with the extravagance of their dinner parties. Alex and I playing dress-up in her mother's vintage Valentinos and Halstons. We were served wine from their favorite vineyards in Napa, where they also had a house, and we were expected to converse. The day after I got engaged to Brad, it was Alex's mother, Linda, who threw us an engagement party. She gave me a lace handkerchief with a card that said, *Something old*. My family wasn't there, but Carly and Alex were. Brad was so blown away; he couldn't stop talking about the house when we got back to New York.

But now Linda is sick. Really sick. Alex has been flying back and forth from her place on Devoe, but she's officially moving back to Los Angeles. Back into Charmel. It was almost impossible for Alex to get information from New York, as Linda has been evasive, proud, and deeply in denial about her cancer. Things are devolving quicker than expected. When I first moved back, Linda was still upstairs in the master suite. Now she's been moved to a hospital bed in the downstairs bedroom with a full-time nurse. I've come over tonight because Alex and I are going to cook all of Linda's favorite foods and have dinner together.

When I get out of the car, I steel myself for the experience ahead. I have some intimacy with sick people, that's not what disturbs me. It's that Alex just lost her father three years ago, in this same house. It's that Carly lost her mom when she was twenty-five. The sigh I heave is for my best friends who are losing their parents: parents whom they missed when they were away, parents who were conspirators in their lives. And my parents—twin vacancies—just keep living. I want to apologize for how senseless it is.

Linda didn't lose her hair. She's the type who wouldn't allow such a thing. While Alex preps ingredients, I sit next to Linda's bed with a laptop and we click through photos of Alex's wedding venue in Napa. Linda nods to photos, indicating she wants me to continue, but doesn't speak. Her breathing is labored, throaty, wet. There are oxygen tanks next to the bed. Her coughing is unlike anything I've ever heard before. Each time I clench my teeth because it sounds so violent shaking her tiny frame. I've mentioned casually—to both Linda and Alex—that we could postpone the wedding that's scheduled to happen in six months. From what I can gather, which is what Alex gathers from doctors who won't make absolute statements, Linda won't make it. *Or perhaps,* I say carefully, *we could do it next week in the backyard?* Linda ignores me. The commotion of planning, the efflux of money, the illusion of control, it all feels like a circus of denial. Busyness that takes away from the gravity of these—almost certainly—being some of the last months (weeks? days?) Alex and Linda have together. Alex sometimes tries to talk to her about it. *Mama,* she asks, *maybe you can give me a sign. Maybe you can tell me what you'd like to come back as, so I can look for you.* She forbids all talk of death. Instead we talk of weddings. Maybe it's better this way. Some minutes later, Linda turns to us and says clearly, *I think I'll wear orange to the wedding. The Carolina Herrera.*

We cook a feast. Steak and chicken. Five different vegetable sides. We have peaches to grill for dessert. We use all the dishes, every cooking surface. There is enough food for twenty. Linda isn't able to make it out. We take little plates into her room and turn on some reality television. Alex tries to feed her mom, but Linda isn't interested. Each breath gurgles in her throat.

Later Alex and I take bottles of wine outside. I eat some of Linda's mushroom chocolates, a gift from some well-meaning visitor early on, and Alex and I accidentally get really drunk. We have a way of drinking with each other, impassioned and inno-cent, and then *whoops*, we're wasted. We strip down and sit in the hot tub and stare out into the night. It's moonless and pitch-dark, a void just beyond the edge of the pool. We talk about Devoe Street and New York and all the crazy shit we used to get into, how the hangovers would last days, but they were our favorite days.

I can't do this again, Alex says at one point. Her face contorts, then she blinks it away. She dislikes crying. She's rational, well-mannered, able to forbid her own feelings the way her mother forbids certain kinds of flowers in the weekly arrangements. I think Alex means she can't watch her mom die, like she did with her father. I don't know what to say. I think back to all the times Alex has picked me up off the floor. When I would tell her I didn't want to continue living, she would say, *You don't have to. You just have to make it until morning.*

We climb upstairs to the master bedroom at two a.m., trailing wet footprints, leaving the kitchen a mess. God, Linda used to scream at us if we left so much as a water glass out. If there was one streak of grease near the stove. I guess it doesn't matter now. An hour after we go to bed, I wake up to Alex moaning that she's sick. I follow her into the bathroom and rub her back while she pukes. I ask if she took any pills and she swears she didn't. I don't know if I believe her. *I'm spinning,* she says. Linda's cough flares up and echoes through the glass house. Alex winces.

I have her lie against me. I sit against the wall with a pillow on my lap and Alex in front so she can be reclined. This is a trick from college. It helps with the spins, as does keeping one foot on the ground, as does not drinking so much. I tell her the story of Dante's *Inferno,* from a class we took together, but I remember very little of it, so it's radically condensed. The thing between Dante and Beatrice is more sexual and less divine. Alex's eyes are closed, and she gives me a few smiles. Her breathing slows and I wonder if I can wedge a pillow next to my neck so I can sleep. She opens her eyes and looks at me.

Where is he? she asks. She means the Monster. He was supposed to be in Los Angeles by now. Alex has enough grace not to ask directly.

Stockholm, I whisper. *A new project.* I give a shallow cry and swallow it, apologetic for the pettiness of my pain, and also relieved to show it.

I'm sorry. I'm sure he's coming.

Linda's coughs are like gunfire. I hear movement in the nurse's room downstairs, a door creaking open, and I'm sure the nurse is giving her a sip of water. But the coughing goes on for long enough that Alex startles when it goes quiet. I try to take deep breaths so she'll mimic me and fall asleep. I think, in that moment, that Alex is the least judgmental person I know. So much kinder than me. She tells me all the time, *We do the best we can with what we're given.*

Long Beach, California

en are cowards, my aunt says to me. *He's not going to leave his wife. Their essence is just scared little boys. He's afraid you'll leave him someday. You think because you had the courage to leave your marriage, this guy does as well. He doesn't and it's not his fault. He's not built for it.*

He's going to leave, I say quietly. *He said before the holidays.*

Are you really this stupid?

Countless times I've washed up on the shore of my aunt's home in Naples and taken refuge. I even lived with her earlier this year, for a month, while finishing one of the drafts of my novel. She deposits me in a massive bed with Porthault sheets and brings me a massive glass of the cheap Chardonnay my uncle favors at 5:30 p.m. on the dot.

I sit with her and my uncle in the evenings and they tell me stories about California. Corrupt politicians, money-laundering schemes on Catalina Island, gossip about Gil Garcetti, famous cases they were briefly custodians of, all the ways the cops fucked up the O.J. trial. We sometimes argue about politics, then pull back before anything becomes hurtful. My aunt does my laundry, chides me for dressing like a kid and for wearing the same four outfits for the past year. *Don't you just want to burn these clothes?*

This must be what people feel when they go home to their parents. I can't talk to my friends about this affair anymore. I'm defensive, self-righteous, a tone I know from when I've been part of interventions. I speak hotly with denial and I don't care. It's a state of mind that is strikingly similar to faith.

My aunt, for whatever reason, from whatever bank of life experience, is kinder about this than about most of my alternative listeners. She actually remembers the Monster. I have no idea why or how, but when I told her I was seeing him, she wasn't surprised. *Oh, he was always in love with you. I could tell by the way he looked at you.*

He was fourteen, I replied. She shrugged. *It was plain as day.*

I've never been able to see anything so clearly, I say. *My life with him.*

You see it clearly because you're making it up.

I'm not stupid. Do you think I would be in this if I wasn't sure?

She considers this. I see her imagining whether she's going to have to have dinners like this with the Monster, see him on the occasional holiday. Or if this is going to be another painful story in my database. The odds, I'm aware, are not with me.

You're going to be broken before you begin. It will all be uphill.

It cannot be harder than what we're doing now. There will be peace. Peace is coming.

I'm staring into my Chardonnay glass. I haven't spoken to the Monster in two weeks, allowing him *one last time* in therapy with his wife. But I feel him out there, circling me. We often said that we would have found each other earlier if I hadn't been sent to Colorado. We often wonder why he walked into Union Square

Cafe in New York City, just three weeks after I had gotten the job, with no idea I even lived in New York. These kinds of stories protected me from believing I degraded myself over absolutely nothing.

Do you ever wish you had stayed married? my aunt asks suddenly.

I guess it's strange I never think about that. *I wish I was the kind of person who could have stayed married.*

I flash the snake ring at her. She smiles. There's a fire in the outdoor fireplace. I can smell the sea. I recalled suddenly my first winter in New York City. I couldn't afford to buy myself a dresser so I lived in a room surrounded by suitcases. She flew out and bought me a winter coat from H&M. She often appeared in moments of believing I had no one. And now . . . she's pleased . . . She's pleased I'm with her, I can tell.

You know, I never thought you'd move back here. Never thought you should go to graduate school for that gratuitous degree. I did not think you should leave your marriage. I don't say this often, but I was really wrong about that whole thing.

What whole thing?

You.

Colorado

Every addict's journey follows the same trajectory. It's an Icarus story: a high that's unsustainable and then down, down, down. Still, I'm not entirely sure what happened next. I was at Kenyon and the news and updates came to me in fragments. I had trouble getting people on the phone. Each time I checked in, the stories of who found out what, what exactly happened, lost the chime of truth when they were repeated.

To the best of my knowledge, he had been behaving erratically with family members and friends for anywhere from six months to a year, depending on whom you ask. This included my drive from Colorado to Ohio in 2005, and could include his disappearance in Rome earlier in the year. It was chalked up to his unemployment.

One of my cousins found my father walking through his house early in the morning, going through the cupboards. He had been talking to himself.

Acting against advice, he sold the Hygiene house for half its value because he needed cash.

He was found in a parked car on my cousin's street, foaming at the mouth, an empty bottle of OxyContin in the center console.

He was in a detox center when the house needed to be vacated. My cousins moved his furniture out into a storage unit. They lifted up the mattress and found dozens of used syringes. That was how we found it wasn't just the pills. He had been injecting crystal meth between his toes.

When this news hit me, the meth, the context of our drive two months earlier finally made sense. It made a nightmarish, incredible kind of sense. The fact that he was carrying on a double life the entire time I was in his care also was—in retrospect—obvious.

What came back to me was a day in high school when I was having lunch with a friend, an insomniac musician who lived down the street in Hygiene. He said, *Your dad was walking again last night.* I asked him what he was talking about. *Your dad walks and smokes at like three in the morning. I see him all the time, even in winter.*

It's only in writing this that I'm disturbed by my ability to deny the truth. Most of the time I wear that ability like a survivor's badge. But I must have known, somewhere, and then decided, a thousand times, to un-know it.

———

There are boxes piled in the garage at Laurel Canyon. In those boxes are broken mason jars, niche cooking equipment like a pickling kit and a pasta maker, notebooks, my wedding dress, and half a dozen impact letters, written at the request of various rehab centers. My mother went twice before the aneurysm. My father, after 2005, would relapse at least once a year for the next decade. The letters have a formula. I have copied and pasted from one to the other, depending on which parent I'm addressing. The times they scared me. How much it hurt to watch them hurt themselves. How alone I've felt, how I've struggled to fill the void they left. How I wanted to believe they could get better (the preferred phrasing is, *I know you're going to get better*).

In these letters, there is a girl displaying how tough she is. She says she expects little, but I know she foolishly hopes for so much. The hope should be honorable. But as I get older, the more it seems like detrimental magical thinking. Every time they did it to me, *again*, I was sliced open, idiotic with surprise: *How did I become so fucking pathetic? How do they still hurt me?*

Because I'm writing about them, I remind myself. I'm in the garage, looking for a notebook from 2005, wondering what was going through my mind when I got into the car with my father. This is not what I want to be doing. I want to write a novel. I want to stop writing things I've only said out loud to a handful of people, most of them paid professionals. *It keeps them too close to me*, I tell my sister. *I'm losing it.* The act of remembering them feels like a betrayal. Telling the truth about them, when I've been trained since childhood to keep secrets, is unthinkable. But in these days in Laurel Canyon, I cannot write anything else.

Grieving the living feels like an infinite state, until you remember that it ends in regular grieving. It happens in breakups, or in prolonged illnesses. It has happened with my parents. As I write about them, they're still living. But they aren't here anymore. We each have our memories, or lack of them, as personal and cryptic as dreams. But we no longer share a history because a history must be corroborated. There is no one to call. There is no guidance, or a center that holds. I think of Orpheus trying to lead Eurydice back into the land of the living, not understanding that she has passed beyond his reach into the realm of the dead. What, exactly, was Orpheus's story after that?

Brooklyn, New York

The day I let my father go was unremarkable except that I was happy. It was the year after his fifth relapse in Estes Park, where my sister and I had flown in. I was twenty-seven years old and newly engaged to Brad. I had never, not once in my life, wanted to be married. When he proposed, I felt shock, then dread, then hope, in that order. His eyes were wet as he held out the ring and I thought, *Why not me?*

Up to this point I had always been involved with my father's recoveries, though I never deluded myself that it was his children that would save him. He liked it when we were there because he liked to show us off, differentiate himself from the other addicts. Still I made space for him in my life. He visited me and Brad a few times, sleeping on the couch in our tiny one-bedroom apartment on Grand Street in Williamsburg.

On those visits Stephen was subdued, chugging sparkling water, but still himself. Boastful, full of stories, preferring to walk the entire city. I was often unsettled when he left. *He's using again*, I would say to Brad after my father walked out the door, and for weeks after I would wait to hear news of the next disaster.

He spoke of having money, though he hadn't worked since he

was fired in 2005, six years earlier. I wasn't sure where he lived back in Boulder, it changed often, but recently he had gotten an apartment with a roommate. He wanted to become a Jesuit priest. He had hiking clubs. Lots of friends. He spoke endlessly about his workout regimen and meditation. He had applied to divinity school. Nothing struck me as entirely logical. I used to say to Brad, *He never really hit rock bottom. I don't mean with his overdose, the car accidents, or poverty. He never let go of this idea of who he was.* Humility was missing.

When I tried to call my father to tell him of my engagement, I was met with a disconnected phone. Not the first time. I tried again the week after. Then I called one of his sisters, who went looking for him. He hadn't been living in that apartment for some time. He'd been living on the couch of someone else in the program, who had since kicked him out. My father was not remotely sober.

It had been a month and we couldn't find him. I sat at the table one night, working on a bottle of wine, and said dully, *He's dead somewhere. The call is coming.*

Brad said we didn't know anything yet. But when I was drinking heavily and could bear it, I could imagine him unmistakably. As if I had a portal in my chest that allowed me to access his feelings. His life was in shadows. He was in places he wasn't meant to be: truck stops, crack houses, empty parks, this golden, graceful man, emaciated and lost.

I saw him begging. I don't mean that he literally begged for drugs, though I know he did beg, and did more than beg, on many occasions. But that each of his movements trembled with desperation, like a trapped animal wanting to escape itself.

I know that as he fell into his black hole, he prayed. Thinking of his eventual death didn't hurt me, perhaps because I had been preparing for it for so many years. When it came, it would be a mercy. The thing I felt most acutely when I thought of him dying, was shame that he would die on the dark side of his life. Not in his home or in the mountains he loved. He would die nameless, in his ghostly world that he could never bring to light.

The end-of-summer Brooklyn light when you live near the water is concentrated and honeyed. Our apartment had only four electrical outlets, the toilet was in a closet, but it was graced with a cast-iron tub in the kitchen. At that point with Brad, it was the longest I'd ever lived in one place since I was eleven. The leaves in the trees outside the window were prolific, almost blocking my view of the East River. I was in a tepid bath midday, even though it was sweltering. Brad brought me a glass of ice water and went back to what he was working on. I watched the beads of cold water drop into the tub and I knew my father was never going to get better. When I let him go, it wasn't in reaction to one of his disasters. It was finding myself in the right temperature, the right light. I suppose it contrasted so sharply with wherever he was, if he was still alive. After all the therapy, rehab, jargon, the quixotic perspectives and contexts that allow us to fidget and escape the logical consequences of action—in my bathtub there it was, suddenly, the truth: it didn't matter.

I'm not getting my father back. Not because he's dead, or because he's an addict. But because he was never there to begin with.

The hardest part of remembering that afternoon is not the loss of my father. It's the way Brad sat on the floor next to the tub and talked to me. It's the bottle of Riesling he opened. He gave me, for our entire relationship, unflinching care. I didn't foresee how some years later I would watch the movers toss boxes roughly. I couldn't imagine I would leave him. I could say I was doing it to be honest or true to myself. That staying in the marriage would have made me a liar just like my father, but in truth, I still have no idea why I did it.

We found my father a few weeks later in a rehab center in Utah. He hadn't been allowed to use the phone. When he finally called me, I didn't answer. I don't know who it was who told him I got married.

The Salton Sea, California

Y*ou wanted conflict,* the Love Interest says, as we contemplate Salvation Mountain. I expect grandeur, but the mountain looks like papier-mâché. A pink, teal, seafoam pile that slides underfoot like melted candle wax. There's a hive of dripping sculptures off to the side. All this absurd color in the middle of a flatland next to the Salton Sea.

The "sea" is still the largest lake in California, called a sea because of the water's salinity. In the 1960s this accidental lake, created from an overflow of the Colorado River and then fostered, was more popular than Yosemite as a tourist destination. By the seventies, flooding from the Colorado River and toxicity in the water threatened commerce. When thousands of fish and bird corpses piled up on the shores, the money abandoned it for good.

Stepping out of the car today, we find the shore comprising pulverized bones and giving off the ironized stench of fish guts. The most prominent and discussed problem facing the area now is that California needs the water it has been pumping into the sea (which also serves as the largest wetland in California, crucial to migrating birds). But without that water the lake recedes, and the lakebed—this one laced with more chemicals and pesticides than Owens Lake could dream of—will become exposed. So the issue comes back to dust. California says it needs the water and does need the water. Water's greatest good, it seems, is to create: build, farm, expand. Water given to repair or maintain a project in its unsexy middle age is always a waste.

None of us ever seems to learn anything.

These aren't really "date" places, I say to him as we get back in the car. The sea and sky are as opaque as a blind eye. We drive past the ruined resorts sinking into the lakebed, and bleached-out signage promising an ocean, waterskiing, a Miracle in the Desert for your uninhibited enjoyment.

We're here for another piece of land art, Slab City, also known as "The Last Free Place on Earth." It's a trailer park of squatters on a piece of abandoned land near a bomb-testing site. It simulates a town, with a bar, a theater, and community meetings. It's covered in garbage, banners, withered plastic, painted pieces of wood with messages directed at Jesus. We are almost out of gas.

We pull out our camping chairs in the parking lot and I open the cooler. A ripe avocado is an optimistic omen in my life, and I have one. It doesn't need anything but salt and lemon. When I open the tortilla chips and beer, two men approach us. One white, wearing thick-rimmed glasses and carrying a twelve-pack box; one black, shirtless, and with pants fallen so low they expose his pubic hair. Both are holding cans of Natty Light. Neither have shoes. Noah, the white guy, introduces himself and his friend, Henry, then they sit down on the ground and ask to *snag a chip.*

It is not entirely true that amphetamines destroy your appetite. You eat not for sustenance or satisfaction but to be doing *something,* whether drinking, smoking, or eating chips—a thoughtless way to tether the mind's mania to movement. The men's hands are filthy, and they plunge them into the chip bag. We all cheers our beers, while the my-little-pony-colored mountain preaches Salvation behind us.

The Love Interest has gone silent. He can't tell if I'm okay with our new, very enthusiastic, friends. He doesn't know that I take a certain pride in being able to pass on the fringes. That I have an expertise in talking to people on speed, or meth, or heroin.

I'm talking with Henry about Slab City, where he's been living for three years. The soles of his feet look like asphalt. Slab City isn't free anymore, at least ethically speaking. It's still a place where you live off the grid, where you barter for goods. It houses a harmonious balance of ex-military libertarians and aging anarchists. *But from an ethical standpoint, it's over,* Henry says, *commodified.* He wants to call his mom and have her pick him up and take him to Detroit. *Detroit is where violence is possible,* he extols. *Violence is the only true expression left to us.* He was a teacher in another life. When I tell him I went to the New School, he talks about Eric Fromm and Hannah Arendt, the German Jewish exiles who taught there during the 1940s. He wants to talk about the Frankfurt School. He picks up the bowl of mashed avocado and helps himself.

Noah recently moved to LA with his wife. He's out here taking photos for the weekend, a budding photojournalist. He asks us, *Were you at Occupy?* and *Why is chaos regarded as a negative concept?*

The Love Interest is watching me. People trickle down the yellow path glazed onto Salvation Mountain and the sun has shifted into its closing stance. GOD IS LOVE is emblazoned on its peak, surrounded by cartoonish hearts. I think about Noah's wife, who is waiting for him back in LA. He has spoken at length about photography, but I've yet to see a camera, or even a phone.

I'm sure he told her he was out for a standard, privileged, voy-euristic gaze at the last shreds of "freedom" and ended up on what was an "accidental" speed bender.

The Love Interest asks if I'm okay. Now I can tell he wants to go, but I smile brightly at him, thinking, *You don't know anything about me yet.* I'm punishing him. For pushing me to talk about people and places I've forcibly tried to bury. For bringing me to yet another godforsaken place. For wanting me to sleep under the stars, to feel light when I arrive at the ever-widening bomb blast of these wheezing desert towns. For a moment, I hate him for not knowing how fragile I am.

I ask Noah and Henry about a gas station and they invite us to stay the night. *Suzie always has space in her trailer,* Henry declares. *It has solar panels.* Apparently, Noah has been there for days. Someone will probably be cooking, and someone will probably drive us into town for more beer and cigarettes and a couple gallons of gas. Their friend Toadie lives in an abandoned water tower, his house is a marvel, we can't leave without seeing it. There's a library in Slab City, a free library in the last free place, I'm told, and I can look at the books.

The Love Interest reaches out his hand. I stare at his palm.

Owens Valley, California

In 2007, my cousin August went into the Inyo Mountains to perform a rite of passage, three days and three nights in the wilderness with no supplies. Though he was strongly discouraged by the family, he decided to stop by the Diggins. A decade after its abandonment by my father's generation, it was covered in five-foot-tall weeds. It was heavily vandalized. The shack had been repurposed as a rat's nest. August and his partner, Claire, spent the summer months camped out at the Diggins, visited by their friends, my aunt, my other cousins, even my father. There were days upon days of manual labor. They rebuilt and replanted. August took over as custodian of the mining claim. He calls what he does out there, "nurturing." He believes our generation can heal that land. I want that to be true.

I'd forgotten about the water. My grandfather was able to build the Diggins because of a pipe that juts straight out of the mountainside. It pumped water—freezing, the color of quicksilver—into a bucket, which we bathed out of, yelling from the cold. The water overflowed from that bucket into a ditch, which we children called "the moat." It encircled the property, lined by thick grass on both sides, a ring of vivid green. The Diggins, our kingdom, fertile, sheltered. Within the perimeter were stands of cottonwoods, apple trees, wild roses, grapevines weaving through an arbor that shaded us during meals. The mountains around us were barren save for some sagebrush and tumbleweeds— a vacant, echoing beige for miles, and then this breadth of green, screaming hope.

PART III

Monster

Los Angeles, California

My grandmother was the first person to confirm my vague feeling that I had a power: I could separate from my sadness. Alchemize it.

We were driving up to Palos Verdes from Long Beach after a day of second grade. I was eight years old. I had written, illustrated, and turned in a story that required my grandmother's presence at school, a substitution for my mother who was always at work. We met with Sister Mary, the principal, and Sister Bernadette, the nice one, and the school nurse. As we drove home, my grandmother asked me to read the offending piece aloud.

In the story, it is an October night. Five girls are invited to a slumber party. Each girl has a defining characteristic: one of them is sporty, one is brainy, one is shy, one of them is the most beautiful and the leader. One of them is the orphan.

During the slumber party the girls play with a Ouija board and detect the existence of spirits. They perform a séance to entreat the spirits to come closer. They perform "Light as a Feather, Stiff as a Board," lifting the Orphan with their fingertips because she is the smallest. All the lights go out and she ascends toward the ceiling. They are successful.

The Orphan drops down to the floor, unconscious. She wakes up and realizes that she is not alone. She has been possessed by an evil spirit, her twin who died when they were in the womb. The Evil Twin begins to twist her thoughts, then her words. The Orphan knows it will make her do awful things, turn her into someone she doesn't want to be. She goes to the kitchen, where the mother of one of the girls is cooking. The Evil Twin tells her to pick up a knife. The Orphan picks it up. The Evil Twin tells her to use the knife to kill the mother, then her friends. The Orphan stabs herself in the chest instead.

The End, I said. I watched for my grandmother's reaction. From this vantage point it doesn't take a psychologist to see how terrified I was by what might seize me. There was already a split in me: disorder, abandonment. I leaned into the gothic to illustrate what I couldn't articulate. At eight years old, I unconsciously understood the function of symbols. I mimicked my favorite writer, Poe, but with this story I had taken the perilous and grandiose first step of making it my own. Did I already know that art could make sense of madness? Did my grandmother?

Her navy Cadillac was at a stoplight. There was a Pavilions supermarket behind her, a row of eucalyptus trees, an air-conditioned stream through the car that made my nose run. She looked at me, so directly I flinched, and she said, *Never stop writing.*

Los Angeles, California

My best friend in the world right now is Carly's three-year-old son, Luca. Though I have always responded to children, the way I feel about Luca is outsized, and probably preposterous. We've grown close in a way I can't justify, as I'm not his blood relative. But I miss him when I'm away. I take note of things throughout my day I want to tell him about, keeping lists of jokes and games. Whenever I leave Carly and Al's house, I'm still talking to Luca in my head. When I'm with him, I don't have to think, or hold myself still until some predatory sadness has passed.

Luca's at the age of imaginative play: pirate battles, great floods, wild storms, jungle animals, and monsters (*Don't worry,* Luca says, *he's secretly a good guy*). We play cop and robber, though instead of the robber, I'm pulled over for speeding on his scooter. We play restaurant, and he's the waiter, the chef, the owner, and they are always sold out of lemonade. I teach him to say, *Eighty-six the lemonade!*

This morning I met Carly at SoulCycle. The instructor blared at us: *What kind of person do you want to be today? A complacent one?*

Or a brave one? I wondered about choice, but I pedaled harder and said back, *I want to be a kind one.*

I've decided not to tell Carly that I saw the Monster last night, or that he's currently at the airport—maybe by now in midair— watching me. His gaze hovers over me, even when he's gone, keeping me inattentive to my real life. I can smell his fear sometimes, that I'll become someone who can live without him. But Carly knows.

Why don't you just stop?

You don't think I've tried? I keep waiting to know that it's the end. For some sign that I'm supposed to give up.

The sign is that you're suffering. There it is.

I know. I can feel myself falling away. I'm scared.

But you're choosing it. You know that, right? That you're making this choice, every day.

I feel choiceless.

Do you know what makes me mad? She turns to me. *That you did it. You fought so hard for this life and now you won't let yourself have it.*

We spend the afternoon with the kids. I take Luca to Rite Aid in his wagon for an ice cream cone. We stand in the toy aisle and I pretend to make a list for Santa Claus of all the plastic crap he thinks he wants. Luca tells me I should marry George and I, having no idea who that is, say sure, he sounds nice enough. We walk back, and the air is damp, spiked with salt. It smells like my childhood.

Epiphanies aren't lightning bolts. They are a hummed note, a prayer mumbled constantly, brought to the surface given the right conditions. It's as if I am always hearing three ways, first shallowly, collecting, then one level deeper as I'm processing, and finally, I am hearing with my body, which is when I'm hearing myself. That's one way, for me, information combines with experience and becomes knowledge. I wish there were a shortcut.

I did do it, didn't I? It's not just a loop of my failures, there is something else too, some remote euphoria that I am a writer. I've forgotten I can choose something else. Forgotten that choice has always been the antidote to fate.

When we get home, Carly and Al are cooking dinner for me. Cacio e pepe, my request, and a salad with blood oranges and cara caras and chicories. There's a bottle of Nebbiolo, but neither of them will think to open it unless I ask them. I will ask them to. I'll only have one glass, maybe a second, but small pours. When I leave, I'm going to drive Sunset Boulevard all the way home. There's a cake tucked into the back of the fridge. I ask them who George is, because Luca wants me to marry him. *Curious George,* Carly says. *The cartoon monkey.* It is my thirty-second birthday.

Since I've started writing about my father and visiting my mother, I notice Luca is the exact age I was when my father left us. That was also the age, three years old, when I had my first panic attack. When I stopped being able to sleep alone in my bed. I watch Luca play and imagine if one of his parents wasn't home anymore. Not living down the street, split custody, alternating weekends, joint holidays, but gone. As in not knowing where he lived, what he did with his days, when or if he was coming back. What confusion, terror, grief Luca would feel. I think it might create permanent feelings of unworthiness in him, believing that he didn't deserve to be loved the way other children were loved. It causes me to cry as I'm pulling away from Carly's house, imagining Luca experiencing that. It's so much easier to have compassion for others than ourselves.

Luca asked earlier if I knew where their cat, Bucky, has gone. I hedged. Bucky is one hundred percent dead. I said I didn't know where he was, but he should ask his mom. Luca pulled my ear to his mouth and whispered loudly:

He's in heaven. But you can still talk to him. You can talk to anyone in heaven.

Wow, I said. *I didn't know that.*

He nodded at me. The most patient teacher in the world.

Los Angeles, California

I remember saying to the Monster when I found the cottage: *We can walk to the Chateau.*

A few weeks before my birthday we walk to the Chateau Marmont. He notes the lack of sidewalks, the suicidal traffic on Laurel Canyon Boulevard. I don't know how to be myself anymore: whether to enjoy him while I have him, to meet his frenzy for me with nonchalance, or to scream at him to respect me, a respect I'm afraid I can only earn by never seeing him again.

I keep my eyes down as the maître d' seats us and recall another night, when he and the servers were background extras in the great romance of my life. The Monster shook his hand, introduced us. We invited him into the conversation. That thrilled me, the public proof of us as an *us,* even if our public was always strangers. That night I had offered the maître d' a taste from our bottle of wine. Tonight, I realize he doesn't recognize us, even as I try to order the same bottle. My wine knowledge annoys the Monster. He believes it all tastes the same, sometimes orders Malbec to annoy me. Tonight, I know there is something vulgar about how careless he is with pleasure. So certain that someone else will pay attention for him.

You've gotten skinny, he says to me. *Your breasts are disappearing.*

The food isn't good, besides the French fries. I explain that I've stopped being able to eat around him because when he leaves, I feel sick. I'm never hungry anymore, and when I eat, it tastes unsalted and ashy. Even my periods have stopped.

The food's never been good, he says.

I don't know. I see, in the distance, my heartbreak blinking, promising a prompt arrival. *I remember it being good.*

We stayed at the Chateau early in the affair, when I was still living in New York. I flew in. I told none of my West Coast friends, or my aunt, that I was coming. Drifting into the city of my birth anonymously elated me and if I'm honest, that's when it started, the splinter of a thought: *I could live here again.*

That time we didn't sleep. *You're a miracle,* he said when he touched me. We couldn't breathe calmly. We touched each other and lost hours. *Can you believe it? Is this real?* Omelets came to the door. He loved to feed me wet foods—eggs, salads, fruit—with his fingers. We laughed at the idea of sitting on opposite ends of the couch from each other, of being able to watch television in each other's presence. *This isn't real.*

Touching lips, *Is this real?*

Hips, *Real?*

We said, *We'll take this slowly.* I wanted to be careful. I was always urging him to rethink things, trying to protect him. My biggest fear, in those days, was that he would leave his marriage impulsively before we knew if this was solid. Then I'd disappoint him. We would become real: I'd nag him about how he washed dishes, or I'd be too tired for sex, or we'd be buying toilet paper together and I'd look at him to discuss what ply paper to buy and he'd be checked out. Worse, I worried that I'd leave him like I did everyone else. I said, *We should wait.*

Tonight, we eat at the discreet tables at the edge of the dining room, invisible. There is a lot of sighing.

We are still waiting. We are junkies who can't increase our dose. Every meeting we're trying to reclaim that brief minute we believed love weighed more than timing, geography, or the limits of each other's character. The same sharp intervals of time, the same inane text messaging, the same replaying and rewriting what we've done, regurgitating excuses for how much pain we've caused, then, the same *someday, soon maybe.* I have never wanted to die more consistently than when I sat through evenings like this, loving him down to his eyelashes and teeth, bludgeoned by that love, while knowing we were rotten.

It is not our playacting a couple to strangers, but in our silence that we can prove any of this was real. That it wasn't lust, or boredom, or pure self-destructiveness, but something spiritual that hushed all other noise. For a moment at least. When the other dies—I pray it's decades from now—will we hold our breath, maybe sigh a remorseful sigh, then rage at someone else who loves us? Will I delete all the unsent letters, accept that I was always talking to no one? Which visit to the Chateau will come back to me?

Sometimes I think, if I had to do this again, I would go to his house after our walk on the Golden Gate Bridge and stand in his doorway while he grabbed one change of clothes. I would take his hand and say, *We are going. Now.*

Touching the nape of my neck, the ridges of my ears, which he notices have perforated edges, *Can you believe it?*

———

Weeks later he comes back. He wanted to be with me at midnight. The first person to wish me a happy birthday. This doesn't land on me as "loving." On this night I single-mindedly resent the space the Monster takes up in my life. He's become a colonizer, someone who declares ownership without concrete investment in the country. He's defined the language, laws, borders. Those borders make the shape of his absence.

I know it's the last time we will ever have sex. He doesn't believe that, but this is—mercifully—one thing he isn't in charge of. It's over.

I don't care, anymore, about the flight he took. The hints, promise-like, but loose enough to slip out of. The false flags of progress he plants as we loop through Fryman Canyon, saccharine light on cattails, another fucking sunset. We sit for a bit on a rock and he is calm, he has everything under control, while I am far away, voiceless, small, but protected from him. *This is it*, I keep thinking. He carries me part of the way on his back, sweat slicking the front of me. I lick it off his neck. We sit in my garden. The Love Interest has installed a fountain, but the Monster doesn't ask where the fountain came from, maybe he doesn't even notice how it obscures the noise of traffic, and we watch the hummingbirds. He looks around when the hills glow and says that he's proud of me. For what, exactly? For continuing to live in spite of him?

Last night the sex was wilder than normal. That was my fault. We've turned out to be pitilessly cerebral in bed. Neither of us would call it "fun." No one laughs, there is no sunshine or indolence. Our bodies ask questions of each other, we tunnel into strange white spaces, time pauses. Once we finish, we're disappointed that we failed to come up with an answer. That rainy afternoon in Brooklyn, when he hoped he would get snowed in but the rain never solidified, he said, *I don't know what I'm trying to get out of you, but fucking is a poor way to achieve it.*

Will you stay? I ask.

He is quiet while thinking about it. Nobody would miss him if he slept over, but I know he's going to say that his coworkers will know if he doesn't come back to the hotel, they'll know and mention something to their wives about how he missed breakfast and their wives will say something to his wife at the next holiday party or whatever simulacrum of bonding his people do, and so he has to be careful. In the next second, he says that almost exactly.

How many times have I told him it was over? A hundred? Told him that I hated him? That he was a coward? A solid handful. Most recently I told him if he contacted me again I would destroy his life. Send the texting transcripts, the hundreds of letters, the pornographic photos, to everyone. The fact that he continued to contact me shows—not that he's fearless—but how little my words mean to him.

I have the urge to tell him that it is real this time. That barging into Los Angeles with gifts and flowers to "celebrate" my birthday and then making me sleep alone is—really, honestly, truly—the death blow to us. But I say nothing about that. He wonders at the fact that I have no curtains.

Aren't you afraid?

I turn to him. *Please. I am begging you to stay.*

He doesn't. I sleep like I have a fever, my skin at first itching, then too raw for the sheets. My earlobes are hot and swollen, I can't bear my head on the pillow. When I scratch my thighs, the hair follicles throb.

In the morning I wake up and sit in front of the mirror we fucked in front of eight hours earlier. It comes as no surprise that I see the Monster in the reflection. It was always me.

Long Beach, California

Another puzzle, another one of Gilda's turkey sandwiches, it's a stunning seventy-five degrees on the canal and my grandfather is wearing pants, a belt, a polo, a cardigan, and thick socks under his shoes. I've decided to interview him. We bypass the morbidity of such a request, and I explain that I'm writing something, but I don't know what it is yet. He hands me a report made by naval officers who interviewed him extensively about the USS *Albacore*, his submarine.

Anything you want to know is in here, and he taps it. *This was a professional interview. The final word on me.*

Right. I take the printed pages that he stapled together. God, I wish I cared about submarines. *I guess I'm wondering about other things. Like your feelings.*

He pretends not to hear me and starts fussing over Gilda. He wants her to sit and listen, and then he wants her to go in the other room and watch television. He wants to know if I want any watermelon with my lunch. *Stop,* Gilda says, *you're always worrying about something.*

Granddaddy, will you just sit down?

He tells me of being fifteen when they bombed Pearl Harbor

and knowing with every fiber in his being that he was supposed to fight for his country. Three years later, he left his home, his violent father (who used a horsewhip on him, also a baseball bat), his band of sisters, and was admitted to the Navy in May 1944, *just in time,* and by that he means World War II wasn't over. When he got to Annapolis, he was a just a poor kid from Rock Springs, Wyoming, where only Italian was spoken in the house. He didn't even know how to swim.

And they pushed you off the diving board, right?

They did. And I learned how to swim real quick.

I know these stories. All the ones captured in that engineering paper.

Tell me about meeting Grandmamma.

You look like her. And a little like me. You get the bags under your eyes from me, like a real Italian.

Thank you.

He can't talk about Grandmamma without tears. *That's better,* I think, then feel cruel. I don't want him to cry, but I don't want his boilerplate either. I'm not deluding myself that we can have some cathartic experience, or that he'll release trauma, or that he holds an answer about these mercurial, self-destructive women who haunt our family. But I am looking for clues.

My grandmother was eighteen years old, trying to be an actress, living with her friend Doreen in North Hollywood. My grandfather and his friend Howard had flown a plane out from D.C., a B-52, and Howard had a date with *this gal, Doreen.* When they went to pick up Doreen, my grandmother came down to open the door. *She had just washed her hair. It was down. She opened the door and I thought, I'm going to marry her.* I know this story too.

The interview rambles: it goes toward Italy, our motherland, toward his beloved sister, Rose, who married into the Mafia, and the Sunday dinners of his childhood, filled with deer, elk, moose, trout, whatever they hunted. I'm frustrated by his lack of introspection. He's not answering the way I want him to; I want answers that reflect myself.

When I ask him if he was ever haunted by the violence of his upbringing, he says, *Of course not.* Learning how to take a whipping gave him his integrity. It's an equation I can't get him to explain: *How exactly does taking abuse equal integrity?* He shrugs and says, *It's real life, honey.*

Toward the end of our lunch, I ask him when he was happiest. He avoids the question by telling me how proud he is to have been in the Navy.

No, I say, *what about your daughters? Your marriage? Your travels? Your grandchildren?* He shakes his head. His daughters didn't impact him much, he explains, it was a different time. I eat my turkey sandwich and turn off the recording, thinking that would probably be hurtful if my aunt or mother ever heard it.

He drums his hands on the table, restless again. Then he says: *I think I was happiest when your grandmother threw parties. When I had leave and got off the boat, your mother—your grandmother— threw us these real big parties. All our friends were there, lots of booze. Your grandmother and I used to dance. Those were really good days.*

I write it down quickly, *He says the parties were the happiest,* and in the moment, I think the answer is hopelessly shallow. The afternoon passes with more disconnected remembrances, descriptions of fighter planes and aircraft carriers and I nod, and nod, and kiss him goodbye and get in his car that I'm still borrowing with its military license plates and then sit in an hour and a half of traffic.

I have no idea what memories will last into my nineties because I have never imagined I would make it there. But on the off chance I do, I'll remember certain meals, perhaps. The din of restaurants. I also enjoy parties. Afternoons of reading, writing, staring out windows as snow falls, melts, picking at my cuticles, lost in thought, then not thinking at all. Strange beds, hard chairs, makeshift desks. Hours on the phone to Christina, Alex, Carly, Eli, all of our absurd gossiping and therapizing each other so meticulously you would think it was a science. It wasn't. It was just nice to be close. Maybe that's what my grandfather meant. I keep turning over his answer about the parties in my head. It was the only sincere, unrehearsed thing he said during the two-hour interview.

California

The Love Interest, during that winter, wasn't much more than California to me: temperate, open space to discover and marvel at, a place I wondered if I could stay. He would see me withdraw and ask where I went.

Have you ever been so scared of some seemingly simple task that you feel paralyzed? Like you're walking from the house to the car, and you can't take another step? I asked him once.

Nope, he said, simply. *Have you?*

Or when you're happy, do you ever feel like it's inseparable from pain?

No. He held my face. I could tell he meant it and he didn't know how to relate to me, or how to respond, so he just touched me. I grew embarrassed.

I let the Love Interest drive, which I don't usually do with men. Today he is driving me to another campsite, Montaña de Oro, which also happens to be five minutes from where his parents live. We are all to have dinner together. I watch the sun-colored black mustard pop off the hills as we pass out of Malibu and into Oxnard, and he tells me how invasive the plant is, how it thrives on newly burned hillsides, how it crowds out native plants and wildflowers.

There are cities trying to eradicate it, he says.

It's still beautiful, I say, *to see it bloom like this,* the hills undulating in front of us, each curve revealing another, through Oxnard and Ventura covered in a mesh of gold.

It is, he says. *But conflicted. Just like you prefer. They say the Franciscans planted mustard along the Camino Real to mark the path. It just happened to destroy the native plant population.*

I'm haunted by the violence at the root of this place. Indigenous people wiped out, land overwritten for profit, this city like none other I could think of in the way it rapaciously took from its environment. It is so plainly unsustainable: we don't even have our own water. One lake after another drained, droughts coming, the fires reignited, oceans rising, and we cling to our routines and arguments. We must believe deep down that we're exempt from consequences. Yet from my limited life experience, I know that we aren't.

Part of me enjoys the contradiction, the beauty, the yellow applause out the window. What kind of person does that make me? I recall another evening the Love Interest and I got into an argument after I realized he didn't know who Tennessee Williams was. I railed against his college education, his fatal mistake of never living in New York City. He felt condescended to, and we found ourselves in our first fight. I did not concede my ground, which was only that I was disturbed I was spending my time with someone who had—literally—never read Shakespeare, but I did apologize for my tone. In the days since, I realized that my disproportionate anger had less to do with the integrity of a liberal arts education, and more to do with the pointless narrowness of my every intellectual pursuit. There seemed to be some slightly immoral trade-off I had made, wherein I'd decided it was worth more to be able to converse about the works of Henry James with, oh, maybe six other people, than to know anything about the physical world besides being able to categorize landscapes as "pretty" or "ugly." When I think of what's at stake in our environment, this trade feels catastrophic. How much of my life have I been studiously ignoring, essentially sleepwalking through? These plants that I thought were markers of spring were, in fact, dangerous.

I touch his neck while we drive. His contentment takes no prodding, does not need to be cajoled or captured. It's evident in his profile, his tan, the Pacific behind him.

You know I just got out of something bad.

He nods. *With that married guy.*

Yeah. Sometimes I'm scared that he's going to leave his wife. And come for me.

The Love Interest smiles at me, and the smile feels careless. *I'm not scared.*

You should be, I say.

Why, he asks, *do you want to be with him?*

No, I say. *It's not that.*

What am I trying to tell the Love Interest? I wanted him to say that *of course* this man was going to leave his wife for me, he was probably on his way this moment. I wanted to give myself an out in case a month from now, six months from now, I had to break off this lovely burgeoning relationship. I could say, *See I warned you, I'm honest, nobody can say I wasn't honest.* I want to say, *I'm scared I won't stop loving him,* or *stop feeling him watching me when we make love,* or *when I touch your neck and think you're beautiful I have to forcibly push back his face, his neck, his smell, swallow some grossly intimate memory that pulses in my blood,* and that *by pushing the Monster away I am always, even in my sleep, fighting with him, and in that way, I'm his.*

Why aren't you scared of anything? I ask finally.

The Love Interest says, *It just feels like a waste of time.*

Practical.

One time after sex, the Love Interest asked me if I was happy. I was so surprised by that question, its baldness, I said, *I don't know how to answer that.* I still don't. Happiness is a filter I apply in hindsight. A wash of color over a span of recollected time. But he is teaching me to name things that move me. Coastal live oaks. Poppies and lupin. Arroyos. When I get in the car with the Love Interest to explore some fabled part of this state, I feel alert, aroused, and at peace. I think this feeling must be very, very close to happiness.

When was my mother happiest? When my sister and I were little, she would speak in French when she didn't want us to understand. We grew up knowing we were Italian, that we had family outside of Turin. The towns my mother's family and my father's family are from are only twenty minutes away from each other (Baldissero Canavese and Bosconero). But France was hers, and she insisted on pronouncing *croissant* with an accent, even at Vons, until she lost that kind of humor.

She had been unhappy at college (*Why?* I ask her on one of my visits. *Were you lonely? Depressed? Homesick?* She shrugs. *I just didn't like it,* and that's it). Other people in the family remember that Nancy was struggling making friends, finding her place. First at Davis, then closer to home at UCLA. She decided to take a year off, become an au pair, and attend the Cordon Bleu culinary school where her hero, Julia Child, had gone. She was—for the first and only time—free of her family, and alone in the world.

Photos show her in groups of friends smoking cigarettes with a sweaty forehead and permed hair. Her recipe books from the Cordon Bleu are handwritten, the paper yellowed now, but one can sense her voice in them, earnest. *The shallot should jump, not spit* or *retain the blood to thicken the sauce, flour never as smooth,* and my favorite, *More butter!!* With two exclamation marks. During this time in Paris she fell in love with an Armenian man who courted her at her local café. Her letters to her mother show that within the year they were engaged, and Nancy would not be moving back to the United States.

The story goes that Grandmamma flew over there to talk some sense into her daughter, but in a twist that reminds me of Henry James's *The Ambassadors,* she stayed too long. Perhaps my grandmother lost her sense of the mission. Granddaddy had to fly there himself to bring both of his women back. They took my mother out of Paris kicking and screaming, forbade her from contacting her fiancé. They put all of her copper E. Dehillerin pots and pans, the tarte tatin mold, in a suitcase so heavy it took two men to carry it. Regardless of how much of this is true, the essence of the story, that my mother was bullied by her parents into a life she hadn't chosen for herself, rings true to me. The copper pans now hang here in my kitchen in Laurel Canyon, tarnished, but as heavy and functional as ever. My mother came home from France, enrolled in Loyola Marymount University, and met my father the next year. So yes, I think that Paris was the last time she was—if she had the ability to be, if any of us have the ability to be—truly happy.

Laurel Canyon, California

Christina flies out after my birthday and from the second she gets into her Uber, she's complaining about the traffic, the smog (*which*, I tell her, *has dramatically decreased since our childhood, yay!*), and general sprawl and disorganization of Los Angeles.

Why? she asks, pulling her bag out of the car, dragging it in the dirt toward the house. *Why, why, why?*

Fleetwood Mac lived here, I offer.

Yeah right, she says.

My sister and I have always been surprisingly close given that we're only twenty-one months apart. When we were young, I was ferociously protective of her in social situations. I bullied girls who bullied her. We played on the same soccer team (she was such a strong athlete she always played up a year) and I chased down girls who hurt her and took red cards for it. We fought the usual amount through childhood; I dominated her until she got bigger than me. I, famously, broke her nose with a golf club, which I maintain was an accident. My aunt says it greatly improved her nose.

But it wasn't until I left California that we developed the bond we have today. We talked on the phone for hours, then would cry ourselves to sleep missing each other. We began to revisit our childhood, noticing we came from a veritable sea of alcoholism and narcissism. We came into a reverential awareness of the insular bubble we created, which was and continues to be so complete that we're still fluent in our secret language.

She's not really here for the holidays. She's here to check on our mother, and maybe to check on me. My sister is in the delusional haze of a fucked-up romantic situation. We talk about it quite a bit. We do not talk about the Monster. I've told her it's over, but she's avoiding it. Christina is a straight arrow, steadfastly honest in her relationships, and my infidelities in the past disturb her, something about her older sister she'd rather not see. The dynamic of our birth order means she's not allowed to judge me. The Monster, the fact that I believe he's my *soul mate*, scares her, probably not dissimilarly from the way my parents' judgment scared me. She also blames the Monster for the fact that I've left New York.

Where's the sun? she asks.

It's three p.m., I respond. During the winter that means light is gone in the canyon. Night is already settling in, aqueous and indifferent.

The next day we talk to a lawyer about a conservatorship for our mother. Turns out, conservatorships are difficult to obtain. As long as Nancy can feed herself, bathe herself, write checks, it doesn't matter that she can't walk, hasn't seen a doctor or left the house in years, or occasionally gets dropped off at a detox center to dry out. Conservatorships aren't for the merely self-destructive. The person in question usually has to be endangering someone else, often a child. And my mother's boyfriend, essentially acting as a caretaker, and at risk of losing his "livelihood," would surely contest it, dragging the process out even more. They're time-consuming, expensive, and very rarely granted.

It's also a lot of work, if you were to be awarded one, the lawyer says. *For you two. You'll be making every financial and medical decision for her. It requires constant supervision. Most often the conservator would either move in or nearby.*

Christina and I share a look that says, *Nope.*

I think, I say, clearing my throat, *we're anticipating more of an assisted-living situation. She can't live on her own and we can't afford full-time, in-home care, and neither of us is able to—*

I can barely say the words—*live with her. So.*

The lawyer sighs a sigh that says she's seen kids like us before, devoted for all of ten minutes before they realize the implications. *The real question you need to ask yourselves is, would she be better off in a nursing home or in her current living conditions?*

Christina and I meditate on that while we drive straight from the lawyer to the Korean spa, the only place in Los Angeles my sister enjoys. We go into the basement where dozens of naked women—squat, lean, breasts that drip toward the ground, pubic hair gone gray, girls who still look like boys—stroll in elegant steam, everyone's skin buoyant.

Nancy's still young. Relatively, I say. I had done a walk-through of a well-regarded and expensive nursing home on the Long Beach shore and been unsettled. Not by the facilities: they were clean, nondescript. It was the realities of senior care that I had a hard time shaking off. I walked in and, as if on cue, a staff member dragged out a mop to clean shit off the floor. A diaper had overflowed in the lobby. There were people being walked, playing cards, watching television, sitting in a courtyard with potted jade plants. Only a few still mobile.

A woman pushed a walker through the hallway with tears running down her face. She looked at me. I paused and smiled. She said, *The world is so ugly.* And then she pushed on.

What would happen to my mother in there? I'm wary of people who retire too young. What little is left of her brain would atrophy quickly in an environment where dementia is the de facto state. It was a place I couldn't imagine my grandfather in.

That's not the only nursing home, my sister says. She's practical and exasperated by my hyperbole. (Once she boiled down all the mythmaking and drama of my adolescence to *I think you just had abnormally high hormones.*)

She continues regarding the nursing home: *They have activities. And she could have therapy. And we wouldn't have to worry if she's eating. She couldn't drink. She could improve.*

She's right. *I agree. I mean, it's not like she's social now. She could be social, I don't know. Make a friend?*

My sister thinks about it. *So it* could *be better.*

Yeah maybe.

Neither one of us believes it. Our mother has always been a paranoid, private person. She's found stability surrounded by her things. Even in her current state she won't let me borrow her vintage St. John blazers or old Jimmy Choo heels, despite the fact that she can't walk and hasn't been out of baggy sweats in years. I don't blame her. Her objects are her history.

Do you think she's happy? my sister asks. *She never calls me. She never asks to see me.*

Me neither. She canceled on me last week. I had already driven to Long Beach and she called and said she was busy.

Doing what?

Exactly.

I don't think my mother remembers how to use words like *happy* or *sad.* Both seem oddly existential and unnecessary to the state she's in, where one day is indistinguishable from the next. Unable to change, she's lost the ability to dream, desire, create. Perhaps she's achieved the presence I crave. If that's what it looks like, do I want it?

I am lying on my stomach, while a Korean woman scrubs me. My face inches away from the inner crease of my elbow, arms over my head, legs spread while she breaks down the skin of my inner thighs, my ankles, my butt cheeks. It hurts but it's a fresh hurt. The skin in my elbow is creped. I'm staring at it, its slackness, a shriveled excess of skin. I'm thinking such insightful thoughts as, *I'll start wearing sunblock*, *does this woman see my vagina*, and I hear a third thought underlying those on repeat, *That's not my arm. That's my mother's skin.*

She's hiding, I say when reunited with my sister, as we apply sheet masks. *She thinks she's hiding the drinking. Like the old days.*

After you left, it was always our secret, what happened in our house, she tells me. *There was so much pressure on me to keep her alcoholism a secret, to let her be a perfect mom.*

A perfect mom? I'm startled.

Yeah, snacks on the soccer field, trips to the mall, manicures, you know.

I don't. She did those things for you, I say. Our experiences of high school couldn't be more unalike. I cried our family's dysfunction at anyone who would listen. Teachers, therapists, restaurant coworkers, friends' parents, my aunt, all were trying to help me. I realize that my mother got to rewrite it all with Christina, who had been trained since birth to avoid conflict. For what it's worth, they never fought. And while I don't begrudge Christina the easy passages of her adolescence, occasionally I want to shake her and ask if she knows how hard it was for me. Once I left, it was like I never happened.

Anyway, my sister says. *Hiding the drinking isn't good.*

I'm trying to make her accountable, I say. *But I'm not qualified to do this. I can barely look at her. I don't know what we can do. Are we really supposed to take over? Stage a coup?*

We can't do it. We don't have any support from the family. Not even Granddaddy. They all think Larry is better than a nurse.

What she doesn't say is that we can't do it because we are kids. That we were never supposed to be doing this. But that's not something we say out loud. She fingers her pores in a mirror. *Frankly, I can't afford it. Can you?*

Of course not. I can barely afford to take care of myself.

Here we are. Two adult women, both married and divorced before thirty years old, high-functioning self-medicators, eternally anxious, with no idea how to trust ourselves. Once, Nancy and her boyfriend got wasted on Christmas Eve and woke us up in the middle of the night to open presents. It shouldn't have, but it felt like a breach of trust. My sister and I both started crying. *It's not the morning,* I said, through tears, pushing the presents away, while they tore at the wrapping themselves. I remember the smell of wine on my mother and how mean her boyfriend was about our crying. I was ten. Who teaches you to trust if your parents don't? When both our parents fell apart in 2005, people would come up to my sister and me at weddings or family functions to tell us how miraculous we were. They were comforted by our youth, by our escape to New York City, by our early marriages. It was only as we grew older, both divorced, that the praise turned hesitant. *Blood is thick,* their eyes say.

I'm getting wrinkles, Christina says, trying to smooth out her forehead. Her skin, at this moment, is wrinkleless but there's no use telling her.

At least you don't look like her, I say, inspecting my own face. Christina's eyes cut quickly around my face. She seems surprised.

Yikes, she says.

———

A few days later, Christina is stoic on our hike through Runyon. I couldn't have produced a more striking winter morning, the kind that makes New Yorkers decide once and for all to quit the city. She won't speak, her hands clasping her phone in her sweatshirt pocket. I stop trying, letting her steep in anxiety over an arrogant *Saturday Night Live* director I deemed worthless a month ago. But she's taking it hard. That he's also in LA at the moment seems to have thrown her off-kilter.

My aunt says that after my sister was born she didn't make a sound for nine months. She slept in a bassinet or watched noiselessly. Of the two of us, she was always considered the quiet one, shy, hiding at the edge of the frame in the videos my grandfather filmed of us. One finger in her mouth, she watches me belt out Marvin Gaye, self-absorbed and tone-deaf. But I know that she stifles her feelings and anxiety. By the end of the day I can feel the tension radiating off her and I ask her what I can do.

I want to go out, she says. She almost yells it. *I want to meet people.*

I cringe. *I don't know where to go*, I say.

Can't you do this one thing for me?

She wants me to call around, find something for us to do.

I can't do that. I only hang out with Luca right now. She tells me to call the Love Interest, maybe he has some friends.

I can't, I say. *I'm trying to take it really slowly.*

You're saving yourself for the Monster? she asks.

It's over. I told you—

Yeah right.

Come on, Christina. Not even my sister, who would follow me into fire, believes me. I can see that she's tired of me.

No, I say, trying to reset. *It's not him.*

Great. Let's go out.

Christina washes her face, first with an oil cleanser, then a foaming one. She tones it, applies an essence, then a sheet mask. She stretches while the mask sits, and I bite at my cuticles, refusing to move from the couch to shower. After the mask she moisturizes, a cream, then an oil. Her skin looks like glass. She sits in front of the mirror and brings out her curling iron, an item I have never owned. She separates her hair into sections and twists them around the iron, her mouth rigid, and lets the curls bounce out. I put on music, then turn it off. My stomach is clenched.

Why can't I do what she asks, when it seems so small? Why does her way of coping threaten me? Why am I so angry that someone hurt her, but I'm blaming her? Why do I want to insist that we cope in my way, which involves building an impenetrable structure around myself that won't allow anyone close enough to hurt me, and does not involve *meeting people?*

My stomach hurts, I say finally. *I'm sick. You can call your friends, but I'm not going.* Her hair is in the kind of loose waves I have to pay someone to perform on me. Her face is impeccable. Then it's a cracking mask.

It's always about you, she says. Then she starts crying. Really crying. *It's about you, and your big feelings, and there's no space for me.*

My sister is the only person I bargain with God for *(You can do anything to me, but please spare my sister)* but when she starts to cry, I do not feel sympathy. I feel rage.

Stop crying, I say.

I don't want to. She cries harder.

Stop it, I hiss.

You abandoned me, she says through her makeup. *You rejected me.*

She sits on the floor as if she's about to have a temper tantrum and sobs. I have no idea how we've arrived here.

Are you fucking kidding me?

You abandoned me when you went to Colorado, and you abandoned me with Nancy, and you abandoned me in New York. You left me alone.

Somewhere in my body there is a puncture, but shock keeps me from feeling the damage. I observe it, but adrenaline has taken over. It's impossible that I made her feel the way my mother made me feel, that I raised her only to hurt her in the ways I was hurt. This can't be the legacy of my love, can it? I don't say any of that.

Get. Up. I say. *And get out of this house if you really feel that way.*

It's what my mother said to me when I was sixteen, right before she changed the locks. Christina cries harder and begs me not to say that to her. I say it again, louder, and pick up my phone to call an Uber. I hold the phone in front of her to show that a car is coming, and she puts her hands over her face, *Please don't do that.*

Why can't I stop? Why is this the part of my inheritance I've absorbed? I look at her and a memory comes back to me, a vision of her at fourteen, in Old Pukey, the Volvo, driving in Colorado. I was talking fast in the front seat, directing her, while she drove. She didn't even have a learner's permit yet. I was forcing her to learn to drive. I wanted her to be designated driver for me that weekend. At the on-ramp to the freeway, she started crying. She told me she was scared. *Don't be a fucking baby,* I yelled at her. *You have to get stronger.*

All my life, I believed I was protecting her by training her. When we were little, I told her we had to be soldiers in addition to princesses. I told her not to let anyone see her cry. Now she is an adult and curled in a ball on the floor because she thinks I'm her parent. She thinks my approval will stabilize the shitty terrain we always seem to be walking. I should say that to her. I should start it with, *I'm sorry.* It's the first time I can feel the magnitude of the disservice I've done her, making her believe that feelings were weaknesses, or that people like us couldn't afford to have them.

At the same time I see that if she doesn't pick herself up from this—if she can't get on the freeway—then she will be a victim. She will be the parts of our parents that didn't survive. But I can't say any of that. It's only clear I care more about her survival than her heart when I say to her: *Grow up. We're all in this alone.*

Then, *I think we should go to bed.*

My sister and I can't help holding each other in our sleep. First our toes touching, then one stomach curving to one back. The next day we go to yoga. Her hair is still curled. Then we go back to the Korean spa and keep trying to be all of each other's family.

Los Angeles, California

I wake up and his lips are on my forehead. I draw back, confused. *Where am I?*

I was checking your temperature, he says. I notice I'm covered in sweat, the pillow under my head is soaked. *You were yelling, No, in your sleep.*

I sit up, irritated. The Love Interest doesn't know how hard it
is for me to sleep at his house. After he passes out, I sneak to the
bathroom to do my idiotically complicated skin-care routine and
then take Xanax or melatonin. He lives near downtown LA, in an
area that I accidentally called "scary" the first time I went over,
and I haven't heard the end of it since. It's MacArthur Park adja-
cent, once the crown jewel of Los Angeles in the 1920s, complete
with rowboats and a bandstand, and surrounded by mansions.
Now I can't walk from my parking spot to the Love Interest's
house without being harassed. The front yards are full of garbage, a few tents lining sidewalks, tarps strung together to create
shaded passages. But the Love Interest knows all his neighbors
and walks his dog without commentary from the entire street,
so it seems to be my problem. A car alarm goes off—every
morning—at six a.m., directly under his window.

I look around his room. A lumpy mattress with what was once beige bedding that now just looks brown, and a spectacular lack of objects. A defunct filing cabinet, a few books from grad school, a photograph of his mother. *This is the room of a sixteen-year-old boy,* I say. He opens the window, where more street noise rushes in, the car still alarming, but I begin to cool down. *Where did you get this mattress?*

He sits back down. *This? Why?*

I don't know, I say, *is it made out of straw? Or cement? Or lumps? Is my mattress made out of lumps?*

Well I know it's made out of lumps, but where did it come from?

He leans back in his bed and pulls my damp body onto him. He whispers that this is his *park mattress.* After he finished working in Alaska as a kayaking guide in Denali State Park, he decided to hitch rides down to San Francisco. He crashed with friends when he got back into town, then found a room in an old Victorian with five other people, a gorgeously crafted house above the Matching Half Café. He found that after living in a cabin in the woods—sans plumbing, showering at the Roadhouse, shitting in an outhouse, hauling water from town on a mile-long bear trail, looking over his shoulder constantly for grizzlies, and hitching all summer—he had no things. And he liked not having things. In a fit of asceticism, he decided to forgo a bed. He slept in his sleeping bag on a yoga mat, with a blanket folded up under his hip. *They were nice floors,* he says, like that matters. He slept like this for months.

You're joking.

Do you want to hear it or not?

He realized he needed a bed when he brought a girl home and she was not into his sleeping situation. Still he wasn't in a hurry. On New Year's Day he woke early, hungover from a warehouse party, and headed out into a sleeping San Francisco for a walk. No one else was out. As he came up to Alamo Square, there it was: park mattress. *In great condition*, he says. *It was a sign.* He ran back home to get his car, tied it onto the roof, and his roommate helped him carry it up the stairs. It has been his bed ever since.

The sun is coming up outside his window and I can see the top of City Hall. The more time I spend with him, the more my skepticism is interrupted by spontaneous bursts of affection. I'm having one now. It comes out like laughter. I can't be close enough to him.

I really like you, I say.

He slaps his hand on his awful mattress and says, *I guess you must.*

———

A nightcap? I ask Eli.

It's Christmas Eve and we are on our way back from Carly's. I impulsively swing the car left onto North Beverly Drive. Eli, I am surprised to learn, has never been to the Polo Lounge at the Beverly Hills Hotel.

We walk through the heady, night-blooming gardens, the air damp with unsustainable greenery. There are people unmoved by this kind of manufactured beauty, but they don't end up in Los Angeles.

The Polo Lounge is strung up with Christmas lights and prostitutes. There are the straggling men who pay for sex on Christmas Eve, and an Australian couple who sing along loudly to the carols the piano man plays. The wife is barefoot, rubbing her feet into the carpet, occasionally trying to get up to dance before falling back into her chair. We order negronis and we're content. We chat with a man in an all-white suit crowned with a black bolero and he tells us stories about fucking transvestites in San Francisco in the seventies—*a hole is a hole,* he says, *and besides she was beautiful.* Eli and I nod, full of understanding. He and Eli get into how degraded the city has become by tech money, the traffic, how *you can't find a tranny bar anywhere.* He buys us a round and invites us back to his room to do *a shitload of cocaine,* which we decline. He moves off the bar, swimming into his endless evening, appearing to be some sort of Messiah, a man totally at peace. As he passes the piano, he turns and waves to us: *Merry Christmas, darlings.*

Eventually Santa comes, another wasted character wearing a suit filled with stuffing, and sits on Eli's lap. They flirt for a bit and I watch the bartenders mix drinks and whisper about the guests without moving their lips.

Christina has flown back to her beloved New York. I spent the middle of last night looking at plane tickets, wanting to head back to Sicily, where maybe I could spend a month in my editor's empty cottage in the mountains. I can see it all, the slow-simmered sauces, the paperbacks piling up as I finish them, the wine bottle suddenly empty, whoops, emails unanswered, some glorious unaccountable aloneness. I'll tell the Love Interest I'll write, tell the Monster nothing, but he'll find me, and I'm so weak that I'll let him. I'll tell my friends I'll miss them. I'll help my landlord find a sublet, pay the new renters to let me store my shit in the garage. My parents will slip from memory, and their tentacles of sadness won't reach me. This is my instinct, with the sheen of brilliant idea. *I'll burn it down,* I thought. *It will be like I was never here. Again.*

And then what? I asked myself.

Santa leaves us, and our tray of corn nuts and pretzels is refilled. I turn to Eli with a completely insane, half-baked idea.

Hey. You know how you hate San Francisco?

Yeah. Miserable.

Do you want to move in with me?

He doesn't bat an eye, like he's been waiting all night for me to ask.

Meh. Into that disgusting closet?

It's technically a bedroom.

I won't pay full price.

Of course not.

There are spiders everywhere, even in the bed.

It's a season here, like a spider season—

I am covered *in bites.*

I'll call an exterminator.

Sure.

Really?

I mean, we are one hundred percent going to die in that house when the trees fall down on us, but you won't have to die alone listening to Adele in your bathrobe. So that's a win.

Cool, I say, half regretting the offer, half moved and tipsy. Did I fail at living alone? Or am I admitting to Eli that I simply need help? My eyes water. I guess I'll try staying.

Los Angeles, California

In 1963, Ed Ruscha put a motorized camera on the back of a pickup truck and drove the Sunset Strip, photographing the blocks, then turned those photographs into an accordion book. It's called, appropriately, *Every Building on the Sunset Strip*. The photos are just that: every building on the Sunset Strip, in all their tackiness and vacuity.

What his project does—slowly—is reveal a kind of purity in these strip malls, fast food drive-throughs, gas stations, abandoned discos, coffee shops, nail salons, music venues, auto shops, strip clubs, bus stops. This landscape does not possess the architectural uniformity that we commonly call beauty. But when I trace the images Ruscha captured, I'm reminded that it's the way we look, how we organize the world and name it, that creates beauty.

This is not a beautiful city. Any beauty found in it is entirely subjective. It requires what the Love Interest once called *desert eyes*. When people ask me what I love about it, I don't say the mountains or the beach. It's the boulevards, like Pico, La Cienega, Lincoln. Streets that are part highway but still saturated with businesses. Streets that crisscross the whole rambling mess, streets you can drive on and watch urban development unfold, settlement upon settlement, until the streets evaporate into the ocean or the airport. Driving what my mom called *the surface streets*, as in *there's too much traffic, let's take the surface streets*, with the windows down, heater on, makes me think this is the only place for me.

As I drive back to the canyon from Carly's on my birthday, the top button of my pants undone, pleasantly satiated, my phone keeps lighting up in the center console. A text from the Monster: *Will you come to SF this weekend?*

The Monster: *I'm sorry.*

The Monster: *Steph.*

Don't, I say out loud. *Do not.*

The Monster: *It goes without saying that I love you.*

Does it? I wonder. Go without saying?

The Monster: *Please?*

Yes, I want to text back.

You make it sound like it's a game, my therapist said.

A few months ago, I was recounting to her the ways in which the Monster had hurt me, disappointed me, failed to show up for me, disappeared when I needed him, lied to me over and over. How he maneuvered his way back in, how cheap his promises were, how he surprised me, made me laugh, how I was the only person in the world who understood him and his unique brand of torment . . . God, I was so much smarter than his wife, who didn't even see what he was doing . . . God, how much more stoically I could bear it, *look how thin I am,* look how I wear it, how could he not be impressed? Things would be different when we were actually together. As I described yet another humiliating abandonment, I started laughing. I couldn't look at her I was laughing so hard.

Are you charmed by this? she asked, concerned.

You don't get it, I said. I stopped.

I remembered—brutally—how I would laugh with my friends when telling them about my father's gout. *You don't get it,* I would say. *It's the disease of kings!*

It *was* a game. One I played well. It rewarded me the less I felt, the quieter I got, the harder I could laugh. If I made the Monster love me, I was lovable. If the Monster could get better, be a good, caring man, couldn't my father also? I was so desperate to control the story, write the ending I needed. This was why the stakes of this love affair were atrociously high. I want to know what "just" a love story is. It's in loving that we learn that our blind spots are nearly always our undoing.

Oh, I said to my therapist. *You do get it.*

No, I say out loud to the car. *I will not.* I erase the Monster's messages, starting the process of leaving him all over again. I don't know how to keep promises to myself. I don't know how I'll heal without him. But I suspect, on this night, for the first time, that I'll survive it.

———

Right after my divorce, the summer in between my two years of graduate school, I walked across Spain on the ancient pilgrimage trail. I ended up walking past Santiago de Compostela, the traditional finish. I walked to the Atlantic Ocean, via the Costa da Morte, the coast of death, past Finisterre, mile one, once thought to be the end of the earth. I walked to Muxía, mile zero, to a church on a promontory, a site that's been mythic since the Celts, and thought it one of the most magnificent places I had ever seen. I could not believe that my feet had taken me there, and was awed by the privilege of walking. My life had become smaller in those forty-six days, my mind more manageable. But I did not feel absolved of my sins. I was not a better person. There is nothing falser to me than a story that ends with catharsis.

Loving liars, addicts, or people who abuse your love is a common affliction, and we are all mostly the same. We have a gift for suffering silently. No one taught us how to trust the world, or that we could, so we trust no one. We've never developed a sense of self.

There is no cure for the Monster, or the black hole. Not falling in love, or becoming a parent, or making money, or working harder.

Boundaries help. It's through boundaries that we construct ourselves, say, *Here is where you end and I begin.* However, while boundaries are powerful, they're unfortunately not solid. They are made in the imagination, and there are inherent flaws in arming oneself for battle in our fantasies. What is shocking isn't that we have lived through the traumas of our lives. The miracle is that we are still remotely permeable.

Washington

Unsurprisingly, my paternal uncle's funeral in Washington State didn't go well. That's not true, I believe the funeral went well. I wasn't there, but the reports came back: the ceremony was thoughtful, and his girlfriend, his AA community, his friends all spoke lovingly. There was a motorcycle procession. Half of his ashes were put into the Okanogan River, and his girlfriend would take the other half to Glacier National Park, where they'd planned on taking a trip on his Harley in the fall. My cousin said that Gloria, my paternal grandmother, was particularly hard-hit. That as she cleaned out her son's rented home, she put on, and wore, his clothes in silence.

It was my father being there that didn't go so well. It was clear to those who saw him that weekend that he was using again. After the services, his three sisters decided to stage another intervention. It was then he told them he would go into seizures in the next twenty-four hours unless they got him new prescriptions. For daily maintenance, he was taking a double prescription of methadone, plus an average of *fifteen Ambien a day*. My cousin Lysandra, God bless her, wrote my sister and me a detailed recap of driving to different detox centers and hospitals. My father's lies fell apart about what and how much he'd been using (in addition to the methadone and the Ambien, there were opioids). Then he stole a bottle of pills off the counter of a pharmacy when it looked like they wouldn't give it to him. He grabbed the bottle and walked away and had to be stopped by security. She and my aunts—and I could hear how exhausted she was—ended up securing him a bed in a hospital and applying on his behalf to Washington State Medicaid. He would go into detox, then a treatment facility.

My cousin: *I'm sorry if this catches you off guard but I wanted to be sure you were aware and wanted to be fully transparent about the situation. I can continue to give you updates or if you'd rather not hear anything more I will absolutely respect your wishes.*

When I call Lysandra, she is still in a bit of shock. I remember that shock. The whole thing had taken on a nightmarish quality as my father's sisters drove across Washington in the night. It took hours. *Welcome to rural living,* she says. I apologize for my father's behavior.

But I don't want updates. I mean it. I don't want to know about his seizures and detox, and I don't want to know what medications he ends up on, the methadone obviously an example of a cure that begets another dependency and another cure ad infinitum.

I don't want the pay phone calls from the rehabilitation center, where my father will tell me how much better he's feeling, listing the minutes of his workout and meditation routines, all the therapy, then the complaints about his knee, how x, y, z has necessitated some X-rays, some intervention, some *surgery* (one of his codes for using), how whatever sober living situation he was in got *toxic* (another code for using) and he's had to leave, how he's a natural leader in his halfway house, or that they've put him in charge of the volunteers at the shelter where he lives because he's *definitely the only one here with management experience.*

I don't want to know what phase of sobriety he's in, or what far-fetched job he's applying for, and I don't want him to email me saying he's gotten an eight-year chip for sobriety *from alcohol! Yay me!* Because that one makes me laugh out loud.

Do not call me twelve times, one after another, on Christmas, until I answer and listen to you incoherently crying, voice distorted with whatever-the-fuck is in your system. To the rest of you, don't call and ask me to fly to Colorado to put him on welfare, or to stay with him for a week to transition him from the halfway house into the real world, or loan him some money after he's stolen or borrowed tens of thousands from everyone else. Don't ask me to listen to the repetitious monologue of optimism that thinly disguises the most profound hopelessness I've ever encountered in another person besides my mother. Don't ask me to hold his hand while he kills himself.

But my cousin doesn't need to hear this. Any of it. So I decline to be involved, and she understands. I'm still holding this line in the sand that feels like the only thing that separates me from becoming him. *Who*, I find myself thinking as we talk about my uncle's funeral, *will end up at my father's? Will I come to him then?*

I hang up with her and pace my house, feeling him out there and the web of his pain stuck to me, and I can't shake it off. I'm deeply aware that this isn't over yet. When I walk into a night with air like jagged glass, I still miss him. I do.

I love him, I told my cousin at the end. *If you see him, you can tell him that.*

Portland, Oregon

In the spring of 2016, when my first novel is out, I give a reading at Powell's in Portland. The reading is full (a mercy), and the front row is filled with friends, my aunt and cousin, artists I've met at residencies. I've spent the afternoon in the café in Powell's, pawing books, the place a mecca I've wanted to visit for years. My name is on the marquee outside, posters of my book cover throughout the store. Not a second of it is lost on me.

Ten minutes into my reading my father walks in. He's oblivious to his tardiness. He walks down the center aisle, searching loudly for a seat, climbing over people and settling down directly in front of me. He's waving and smiling. It's the first time I've seen him in almost seven years, and the first contact I've had since I published an essay about his drug addiction in a national magazine.

I don't even so much as take an extra inhale while reading. I'm struck numb and I don't remember the rest of the reading, what was asked, what was answered. As the booksellers lead me to a table for signing, one of them waves at my father. I'm confused. The bookseller says, *Your dad is here.*

You know my dad? I ask.

He comes in all the time talking about your book. He's so proud of you.

The other bookseller says, *You're named after him, right?*

I laugh. My father knows I would never make a scene. He knows I'm a ruthless performer of likability, chanting *Everything is fine, everything is fine* under my breath. The child in me is touched that my dad knows I wrote a book. I wonder if he read the essay, or my book, if he thinks I'm smart, how many days sobriety he's telling people he has, and I wonder about the *true* number of days, where he lives, how he pays for things. I think how satisfying this must be for his ego, how he walks around Powell's with a confidence I can't even impersonate. Then I look up at the line of people holding my book and think, *Wait, this isn't about him.*

I'd had another surprise guest at my book launch a month earlier. It was in New York City. Carly and Al had flown out and brought Luca, who ran into the Strand the day my book was released and jumped up and down when he found it. He took the book up to strangers and asked if they knew about it. When I arrived at the Strand a few minutes later, the booksellers were calling Luca my "hype man." He ran to me, hugged me, and said, *Do you see? Do you see your book?* I think this is what it actually means to be proud of someone. But Luca wasn't the surprise.

That night, with my hair blown out, lipstick applied, reading for far too long because it was my first time, voice quaking while answering questions, I looked out: there was Alex, only three weeks after her mother passed. She held hands with Carly, who sat next to my sister, who rested her head on Eli's shoulder. I'm not making this up: I am humbled by this kind of love. Then I saw the Monster in the crowd, grinning. He winked at me, then disappeared. *There you are,* I thought, as if I had seen him yesterday. There was more contradictory feeling in that second than in entire months. I was ashamed: I felt a tense fist in my chest and it still felt like home.

Never mind that seeing the Monster or my father might have upset me. Never mind that these celebratory professional milestones were achieved, not with their support but in spite of them. I've loved some very sad people in my life and hurt myself trying to get them to change. They didn't, and I have no business being surprised by it. People will tell you who they are. It takes an emergency for some of us to listen.

Long Beach, California

Another afternoon I'm sitting with my mother, watching the clock until my hour is up, guessing at traffic patterns, estimating that, with each passing second, I'll sit on a freeway for two hours instead of the forty minutes it took me on the way down.

I haven't minded the traffic, I say out loud to her, for no reason. After so many years on the subway I'm elated to see the sky. To sing out loud to music, make phone calls. It's all stalling to me, these months, this life, sitting on the freeway afraid to move forward or backward, hoping someone will save me, but knowing that no one is coming. *You have to make a change,* I used to say to the Monster. Now I say it to myself. Sometimes I'm commanding myself, other times I'm begging.

My mother looks at me, the same empty look, the same eyes underneath that I think are the most beautiful eyes in the world.

I don't drive, she whispers. She shakes her head, scared of the thought of it.

Nope, you don't drive anymore.

I ask her if we can take down a hatbox on top of the bookshelf, filled with photographs. When I pull it down, a skein of dust comes with it. Inside this hatbox are all the memories that remain of my childhood. I sit next to her on the couch and pass her photographs, silently at first, until she says, pulling the picture close, *Cortina.*

It's a photo of her and my father on skis in front of a mountain. They are small and blurry, but there's my lanky father, and the tiny bird of my mother. The photo is from 1979, five years before I was born. She would have been nineteen and they would have just met.

You skied the Alps? I ask.

She nods, not thinking too hard about it. *Your father was a great skier.*

You were a great skier too. She taught my sister and me up at Mammoth Mountain, a resort that crowns the Owens Valley. She took turns with each of us on the bunny slope, guiding us with her skis around ours. When I remember it now—what possessed a single mother to travel alone on a ski trip, with all the gear and baggage, the boots unclipped, re-clipped, and our endless complaints about the cold?—I see how her children gratified her. We climbed all over her, bringing back our discoveries and questions, and I can still hear the enthusiasm—before the coma changed her voice—*Oh my goodness what did you find?* When I remember it now, she levitated while she skied. A nonchalant fearlessness that she never demonstrated anywhere else in her life.

Who taught you to ski? I ask, but she doesn't remember. She points again to the photograph and says, *Your father called Christina "Cortina." We were very happy on that trip.*

My father did call my sister Cortina. He continues to. I never once connected it to Cortina, Italy, or thought he could be making a reference to a happiness that only he and Nancy would understand. I'm moved.

We keep going through the photographs, but I don't get anything else insightful or new. She points out her clothes: *I made that by hand.* Or *My first Chanel purse.* Each photo I pass to her I wonder if she can see, *really* see or connect to the sense of possibility she once had. I tell my sister I don't know why I'm visiting her—I'm sure guilt is a massive part of it. The longer I'm here in California, the more I'm forced to be honest about how much I want from her. And how impossible it is. Today I realize why I keep returning to this distressing house: I want an answer.

As she holds a baby photo of me, I ask, *Mama, how am I like you?*

She looks alarmed, as if I'm slow. *You look just like me.*

Anything else?

She concentrates. She thinks I'm quizzing her, but I'm serious. *Tell me what's going to happen to me,* I think.

Her eyes land on her books. *You love to read. Just like me.*

I nod. It's enough.

Before I go, I pocket the photo of her and my father in Cortina. I check her trash can and there are empty wine bottles, beer cans. She's not even pretending. I check the fridge and there is a container of tuna salad.

I always loved your tuna salad, I say.

On Triscuits, she says. I'm glad she remembers.

I am aching already, abnormal for me. Usually it's days later, sometimes months, when I'm at dinner, or with friends, or listlessly walking the aisles at the grocery store that I find it unacceptable, *inexcusable,* all the life I've had the privilege of living that she never had. No solo travels in her thirties, no expendable income, no graduate school, no time for anything close to self-realization. She was so busy surviving, and then it was gone.

Perhaps I am like what she could have been like. I take her hand and she allows it. She smiles at me.

You're so pretty. You ended up so pretty.

I thank her and tell her it's because she's so pretty. I ask her if she wants to leave this house. Or leave Larry. Or change her life. She pulls her hand away from me. She shakes her head.

I'm not going to leave this house again.

I haven't cried in front of her in sixteen years except when she was unconscious. And I can't do it now, but hearing her say that breaks my heart. My hopelessness has passed beyond feeling to fact.

That's too bad, I say. I'm thinking, *I have to let you go again. I can't stay here with you. I'll drown.*

She shrugs. Looks out the window and, I imagine, doesn't miss the streets shrouded in a morning marine layer, or oil islands offshore, or the canals too much. It's impossible to know if she's thinking about what I said, but she might be because she has turned to me and says, sighing, *This is just how things ended up for me.*

Los Angeles, California

It turns out that quaint Seal Beach is one of the more pol-
luted beaches on the Southern California coast. The beach
catches runoff from the San Pedro Harbor, the Los Angeles
River at its terminus, and freighter pollution from the port. Seal
Beach is also where the San Gabriel River empties into the sea.
Growing up, the kids all got staph infections if they swam after a
rain. Couches, syringes, old appliances washed up like beached
whales. *Disgusting,* I used to say to my new friends in Colorado,
then Ohio, then New York City.

But that wasn't the truth, was it? Children who grow up close
to the ocean know about freedom. When I started middle school,
I was allowed to get to school on my own, which is when I got my
Gravity longboard. I carried it around between classes or hid it
in the bushes outside school. I skated up and down the numbered
beach streets in a bikini, blessedly unaware of my body for the
last time in my life. I climbed the sand berms the town built for
winter storms and watched the sunset by myself, learned how to
feel small and holy.

When we were kids, we ignored the rivers. There's nothing
more sterile than a cement "flood control channel," a thin stream

of water trickling on, exhausted. But in the eighteenth century the Los Angeles River was an Edenic wonder, surrounded by floodplain forests and wetlands. It was called "the upside-down river" because it had no obvious head, appeared to be *causa sui*. The runoff from the Santa Monica and San Gabriel mountains ran down into the San Fernando Valley composed of porous rock. That rocky soil acted as a natural filter, sending water to an underground reservoir, which then reappeared as a spring in the valley. Spanish explorers noted the proliferation of wildflowers, grapes, roses on its banks. Most Native American villages in this area were built within a mile of the river.

It used to rain here. Los Angeles was known for its deluges and subsequent floods, which wrecked subdivisions, revised the streets. A friend's mother, now passed, grew up in Atwater Village during the 1930s and said in elementary school they went to view the engorged Los Angeles River (I believe this must have been during the flood of 1938, so ferocious it wiped out bridges) and there were dead bodies roaring past. This was shortly before the city decided to "build out" the river, so they could control the floods and continue housing development along its banks.

During one such flood, in 1825, the river broke its banks, destroyed a pueblo, and cut a new channel directly south. It used to empty in Playa Vista, now the end point of the Ballona Creek. Ever since that 1825 disaster, the Los Angeles River has flowed south, re-making the South Bay peninsula I come from.

Today the river is a source of interest, investment, and debate in Los Angeles. The first time the Love Interest said he wanted to take me there, I thought, *no thank you*. But he's been working on projects around the river since graduate school and has watched it change in thorny ways. With the virtuously intended creation of public space—channels of transportation like bike paths, remediating the soil at abandoned riverside industrial sites that could become parks—comes the wrecking ball of real estate interest. Condos will soon line the river. Already there are a few cafés for bikers. Urban planners are talking about the kind of growth for the LA riverfront that makes one fear for the existing communities. Yet they are also re-naturalizing the river. As we walk one afternoon, he nudges me down the cement incline and I hesitate.

I don't think we're supposed to go down there.

It's just a river, he says.

The rivers in LA aren't rivers.

In a stretch between Griffith Park and downtown Los Angeles, called the Glendale Narrows, there is already progress. The gradual recovery of a riparian habitat with arroyo willows and western sycamores, and of a freshwater marshland. There are proposals to change the water allocation, reconnect the river with the floodplains, so that water can be infiltrated back into the earth as opposed to running straight out to sea.

People already kayak here, he says.

Yeah fucking right, I say.

We walk carefully through rocks and weeds, the river bottom soft beneath our feet. There are cottonwoods in front of me, water splitting instinctively around islands. It's spring and the grasses are lime green. There are birds, not just pigeons, but herons, pelicans, ducks as well.

Ducks! I yell.

Ahead are a group of four Chinese men in lawn chairs, feet in the water, fishing. Why do we continue to love this fading world? It looks—for one moment before I dissuade myself—like a real river. An entire river changed course. I'm myopic sometimes.

Los Angeles, California

Three years after my first winter back in LA, in 2018, I woke up at 5:30 a.m. to my blanched gray bedroom in Echo Park and said, *I don't feel well.*

Matt said strangely, *You dreamed you were pregnant.* I couldn't tell if he was asleep. Had I dreamed that? Had I said that out loud? He said again, *You're pregnant.* The drugstore opened at 7:00 a.m. We stood outside at 6:55, waiting for them to unlock the doors.

I peed on a stick, saw two blue lines, and I was pregnant. A formula with the unfriendly bluntness of a math equation. I dislike math, and anything you can't get out of. I stared at the pregnancy test. Disbelief hedged in my mouth. *How?* Isn't this what we wanted and planned for? Didn't I do all the acupuncture, take the vitamins, do the hard bargaining and wishing? I had been told it wouldn't happen like this for me—quickly, or easily.

An hour later, the initial shock fading, I felt a loss. It came in the form of, *I can't kill myself.* It wasn't a longing for death in that moment, but a longing for a longing, which is equal parts nostalgia and grief. Those interminable drives, fogged with depression or mania, where my breathing matched the mantra, *I can die, I can die.* An assurance passed down to me from my mother, who believed in verbalizing her desire for death even when I was a child. Upon losing the ability to fantasize about dying, I saw for the first time that there had been something tender in my attachment to it—it was something that was *ours.* I understood that when she said it, she'd meant only kindness.

It was gone. No exit on my own terms. None of my elaborate escapes. Behind me were a mess of plane tickets and sublets, affairs that ejected me from relationships, the severing of communication with people who hurt me, namely my parents. Ahead of me, a child. I would just have to take it all, whatever the gods saw fit to give me. *I am thirty-four years old and, for the first time, bound to my life.*

———

It was not obvious there would be a baby. I had been pregnant, accidentally and unfortunately, three times before: an ectopic pregnancy that landed me in the hospital for a week and took my fallopian tube with it, a miscarriage, and a termination. I had never wanted children—not when I was a teenager, nor when I was married. I wanted to write, travel, and have enough money that I could pull out cash from an ATM without checking my account balance, simple goals that a baby would complicate. And in my younger, flippant tone, I would say I had no interest in passing down the damage I inherited to the next innocent victim.

I slept with my mother, in her bed, most nights until I was ten. One morning, I would have been five or six, I held her face and told her how much I loved her. I did, it was as natural as breathing. She looked at me and said, *You won't always.* I didn't believe her. She said that someday I would tell her that I hated her. That was how it always went between children and their parents. I could not comprehend it. I remember crying at the time, asking her to tell me it wasn't true. I would have forgotten it if not for the day, nearly a decade later, I first told her I hated her. She smirked at me—and this feels unforgivable when I remember it—and said, *I told you.*

When I said I didn't want children, what I understood, far ahead of time, was that to love a child is to guarantee suffering. There was no way to protect yourself, or them.

And yet all the excuses I gave my partners in defense of child-lessness came to pass: I wrote a book. I traveled. I wasn't working in restaurants. I learned to take care of myself: I stopped losing my jewelry, wallets, cell phones. I had health insurance (most of the time), paid my taxes on time (most of the time).

With age came not self-knowledge but the ability to give myself things, to actualize ideas, to create. That is the power of adulthood I didn't imagine, and it's a hard-earned privilege. It wasn't a biological clock as much as some measure of emotional maturity that let me know that I could—if I wanted—take care of a child. That he or she would never—if I could help it—feel unsafe the way I did.

I realized that the reason I didn't want to have kids wasn't that I was selfish as I always assumed. It was the same reason my mother tried to distance herself from my obliterating love for her, the same reason she prophesied pain for us: fear. I was scared.

The Love Interest became Matt: slowly, with some stumbling. We accumulated tiny building blocks of trust until the two of us together became the thing in my life I wanted to protect. Was the baby simply a matter of finding the right partner? Yes and no.

At ten weeks I lay on my back in a dark room and waited for my old Irish doctor to come in and tell me whether this was real. I had been quiet on the drive, tearing into my cuticles in the waiting room. *Probably ectopic*, I thought. *Or no heartbeat. Or just nothing where there should be something. Let's get this over with.* These are the kinds of things in my wheelhouse. Deep disbelief that I could deserve something that was simply . . . good.

There was a whitish whisper on the screen as the doctor moved the ultrasound wand over my lubed-up stomach. He held the wand still and I looked at Matt because I was scared to see that something was wrong. Matt's face was wet-eyed, open-mouthed delight. I turned to the screen and then asked, *Is it in the right spot?*

The doctor said, *Yes, it's viable.* Then looking at my face, said more warmly, *It's in the perfect spot.*

I saw the baby move and I cried out. It was real, and I held it inside me. Its heartbeat ran concurrent with mine, they mingled, merged. I struggled not to embarrass myself in front of the doctor.

So this is joy, I thought. *I—truly—had no idea.*

When I looked back at Matt, there was a pang in me, sharp, which I can only call envy, that our child got him as a father. There are fathers who lie, disappear, and abandon. Our child will never know anything about that. I have made so many mistakes. But not this. This part I did right.

We don't receive the things we want because we deserve them. Most of the time we get them because we are blind and lucky. It's in the act of having, the daily tending, that we have an opportunity to become deserving. It's not a place to be reached. It is a constant betwixt and between. It's in that hollow, liminal space that I think—*hope?*—humility can be achieved.

Los Angeles, California

Writing is as close as I'll come to resurrecting my grandmother, my mother, my former selves. I can send myself back to the night of my thirty-second birthday, to the woman driving on Sunset Boulevard, back to that original list of things I thought I knew but did not know. It's an anomalous place, Los Angeles, fragrant with exhaust, dust, faint chlorine. They almost changed the name of the city back in the 1880s because it sounded *too Spanish*. It's a name that invokes the heavens, those who ascend and those who fall. Historically, this city doesn't have a shred of self-protection when up against a short-term interest.

Another time in my life I would have pressed into the curves on Sunset, sped up on the turns up in the Palisades, where Sunset is still wooded with eucalyptus and the occasional redwood. It's there you can feel the history of this boulevard that started at Union Station downtown and traced the base of the Santa Monica Mountains all the way to the sea. I would have refused to slow down where the traffic got heavier in Brentwood. I would have switched lanes without signaling, weaving through the other cars piloted by people who drive by riding the brakes.

I think I was once proud of this kind of driving. Proud that I could not imagine my life past thirty, that I still can't imagine my life past forty. I have no example of how to preserve my skin, my wealth, my friendships, my lovers, or myself. And while this darkness chases me, spurs me to drive faster, tilts me toward anything that will hurt me, wants me to shut my eyes and say *I give up*—I find I have made it back to the falling-down cottage that is my own empty house.

It has been so long since I heard from my parents on birthdays. That's fine, I'm not a kid anymore. But I think about my mother, asleep down in Long Beach, her forgetful breathing, and maybe she can barely detect that this day is an anniversary of something she once held so dear. And I think of my father, far from his beloved Colorado, at the foot of another set of mountains, walking during twilight, his legs restless, and maybe he too, feels this winter day is more tender than most. They don't think of me, but maybe, unbidden, they think of each other. It is, after all, the day they became parents.

Here I am, a thirty-two-year-old woman, ambulating between the fatalistic tenet that nothing I do matters, and that—perhaps, terrifyingly—everything I do does.

What if I could be kind to myself? Turn this one corner? *What else*, I wonder, *is possible for me?*

I regret telling my sister that we're alone. That's a lie and it keeps me from wanting too much from other people. On this night, I'm surprised by my desire to cut out my cynicism and pride. My coping mechanisms—the denial, compartmentalization, dissociation, the cringing hope—are tired. I'm flattened by the urge to call Christina and tell her something I've been ashamed to say for my entire life: *It's not fair. It's not fair. It's not fair.*

I would love to tell her something inspiring and prescriptive, but I lack the wisdom. I can tell this story: I have to believe it's possible to be a victim and not live a victimized life.

It's not because I'm clever that I've avoided addiction, or shakily scaffolded a life that may hold me for a while. It's because I love these people, whose texts roll in all night. The love is risky, it opens me at an unhealing wound. If Carly is right and our souls come back to this earth after we pass, and we choose how, when, and why, I would choose this—with my parents, lovers, and friends—again and again.

That is one reason I will not end up like my parents. And yet I live the way every recovering addict in the world does: one day at a time.

You have to make a change, I say out loud to the canyon, the crickets, the traffic, the smog, the coyotes, and that stray cat I haven't seen in a week. *Thank you,* I say to the car.

I think I'm learning how to be careful with things. By *careful* I don't mean caution. I mean it literally, taken as its suffix and root. I am learning how to be *full of care.*

Afterword

Once a month, when we're living in Los Angeles, I take Matt and my son, Julian, down to Long Beach, and we visit my mother. Until I call to remind her we're coming, she doesn't seem to remember she has a grandchild. She does not call me or ask for photos of him. She doesn't even ask for these visits. She watches the baby with fear and curiosity. She's never sure how old he is and is not able to hold him, but when he's there, she doesn't take her eyes off him. These visits are heavy for me. Her condition since 2015 has not improved. She continues to drink. She has not left her house. But we go because it's obvious that seeing Julian brings her joy. She wants him to call her *Nonna*, and we will make sure that he does.

My father came to meet his grandson right after Julian was born. It was the first deliberate visit between us in a decade. What either of us is capable of remains a work in progress.

I do this because I don't believe my son has to inherit my feelings about his grandparents. This story will keep changing as life has its way with all of us. We are still taking each day as it comes. And gently.

Los Angeles, California, 2019

Acknowledgments

When I first published writing about my father's addiction, the response from readers was powerful and at times overwhelming. Thank you for sharing your stories. This helped me believe I could write a book, even without having answers.

I'm deeply indebted to the people who make, read, and love books. Thank you to the booksellers and independent bookstores.

This book took massive reserves of guidance and trust. I am blessed with brilliant, generous readers, and the wisest counsel. Thank you:

To Mel Flashman.

To Peter Gethers.

To Claudia Herr.

To Robin Desser and Sonny Mehta.

To Paul Bogaards, Emily Reardon, Janet Hansen, and the team at Knopf.

To Angelina Venezia and the team at Vintage.

To Jordan Rodman.

To the team at Janklow & Nesbit.

To Adam Ross.

To the editorial staff of *The Sewanee Review*.

To Lauren Mechling.

For the gift of time and space, thank you:

To Antoine Flochel, Alexander Maksik, and the Can Cab Residency.

To Heather Lazare, Chelsea Lindman, and the NorCal Writer's Retreat.

To the readers, artists, and friends who were instrumental to this book, who have made me a better thinker and human, thank you:

In particular to Stuart Zicherman.

To Sarah Esberg.

To Ester Bailey, Ari Basile, Lucia Baskaran, Michelle Campbell, Denise Campono, Joshua Close, Francine Conely, Megan Conway, Mani Dawes, Cindy de Castro, Patricia Escalona, Melissa Febos, Linda Grey Heitz, Elise Hennigan, Dave Peterson, Ella Purnell, Lilli Sherman, and Matthew Strauss.

To my *Sweetbitter* writers' room family, superb teachers each and every one, thank you.

To my Wild family, for giving me safe harbor, thank you:

To Leslie, Mel, Crystal, Kevin Milne, Nali Milne, Indie Milne, Debbie and Sandy Schner.

For the wisdom and unconditional love that permeates this book, thank you:

To my Mannatt aunts and cousins: Marie Mannatt, Kathleen Sapp, Wendy Goldmark, Methea Sapp, Lysandra Donigian, Soren Jensen, James Jensen, August Jensen, Sophia Jensen, all their partners, and the next generation of cousins.

To my aunt and my uncle.

To Eli Bailey.

To Carly de Castro.

To Alejandro de Castro.

To Luca, Francesca, and Emilia de Castro.

To Alex McKenna LeClair Grey Heitz Close.

To my grandfather, James Vercelli Ferrero, Jr., and my grandmother, Margaret Barton Ferrero.

And finally, thank you:

To my father, for the mountains.

To my mother, for Disneyland.

To my sister, Christina Mannatt Strauss. I would do it all again, as long as I'm with you.

To Matthew Wild, the best thing to ever happen to me.

To Julian Wild, thank you for choosing me.

ALSO BY
STEPHANIE DANLER

SWEETBITTER

Newly arrived in New York City, twenty-two-year-old Tess
lands a job working front of house at a celebrated downtown restaurant. What follows is her education: in cham-
pagne and cocaine, love and lust, dive bars and fine-dining
rooms, as she learns to navigate the chaotic, enchanting,
punishing life she has chosen. The story of a young woman's coming-of-age, set against the glitzy, grimy backdrop of
New York's most elite restaurants, in *Sweetbitter* Stephanie
Danler deftly conjures the nonstop and high-adrenaline
world of the food industry and evokes the infinite possibil-
ities, the unbearable beauty, and the fragility and brutality
of being young and adrift.

Fiction

VINTAGE CONTEMPORARIES
Available wherever books are sold.
www.vintagebooks.com